Step by Step Guide to
Meat Cookery

Audrey Ellis

HAMLYN
LONDON · NEW YORK · SYDNEY · TORONTO

Acknowledgements

The author and publishers would like to thank the following for their co-operation in supplying photographs for this book.

Argentine Beef Bureau: front cover, page 57
Fruit Producers' Council: back cover, pages 47, 60
New Zealand Lamb Information Bureau: front cover (step by step pictures), pages 27, 44, 64
Alcan: page 37
Colman's Mustards: page 40
Fatstock Marketing Corporation Limited: pages 23, 31
Gale's Honey: pages 51, 73
Grants of St James's: page 63
John West Foods Limited: pages 55, 61
Kellogg Company of Great Britain Limited: page 43
Lea and Perrins: page 52
Tabasco Pepper Sauce (Beecham Foods): pages 19, 71
The Tupperware Company: page 68

HOME ECONOMISTS
Christina Pitman
Anne Gains

The front cover shows step by step guard of honour (see page 64) and roast topside of beef with Yorkshire pudding (see pages 9, 10).
The back cover shows roast pork with carnival apples (see page 62).

Photographs by Roy Rich (Angel Studio) and John Lee
Illustrated by Tony Streek
Props used in the photographs kindly loaned by Habitat, David Mellor and Harvey Nichols

The author and publishers are grateful for the advice of Mr. S. J. Mallion, SRSH, M.Inst.M., F.Inst.R., the Head of Smithfield College.

Published by
The Hamlyn Publishing Group Limited
LONDON · NEW YORK · SYDNEY · TORONTO
Hamlyn House, Feltham, Middlesex, England

© Copyright The Hamlyn Publishing Group Limited 1973
ISBN 0 600 38024 6 (US edition)

Printed in England by Cox and Wyman Ltd, Fakenham

Contents

Introduction	4
Useful facts and figures	5
Glossary of terms	6
Basic methods of meat cookery	8
Herb and spice seasoning guide	11
Utensils	13
Bulk buying for the freezer	15

Veal
How to choose	17
Offal	17
Chart of cuts	18
Cooking methods	18
How to carve	20

Beef
How to choose	21
Offal	21
Cooking methods	22
Chart of cuts	23
How to carve	24

Lamb
How to choose	25
Offal	25
Chart of cuts	26
Cooking methods	26
How to carve	28

Pork
How to choose	29
Offal	29
Cooking methods	30
Chart of cuts	31
How to carve	32

Cooking for the family	33
Cooking for company	49
Blender pâtés	65
Lone cook	66
Twosome specials	67
Invalid dishes	69
Marinades and stuffings	70
Sauces and soups	73
Garnishes	75
Wines for the table and meat cookery	77
Index	79

Introduction

A joint of juicy, tender roast beef on the Sunday dinner table is still every housewife's dream and, if she achieves it, her pride. But today this is more often a matter of luck than good judgment. Few women know how to recognise good quality meat, or how to cook it to perfection. Fewer still know how to make delicious and appetising meals from the cheaper cuts.

Of all the culinary arts, that of meat cookery came the nearest to being lost during the war years of scarcity. Rationing robbed a whole generation of women of the chance to learn how to pick and choose between expensive and economical cuts; to consult the butcher as a skilled adviser on a good cut and the way to cook it; to compliment him on last week's success with a roast, or complain about braising steak which did not (as the cooks of my childhood used to say) eat well. The butcher was once a valued friend and ally of every careful shopper; and provided you don't ask his advice when he has a queue waiting to be served, he is still eager to help you. If you prefer the less personal service of the supermarket rather than that of a local butcher, you will find this book especially valuable.

Considerable expertise is required in judging meat since many cuts appear very similar, and to the inexperienced, even the meat from different animals looks the same. Mistakes are costly, as you have probably already learned, because with the sharp rise in cost over recent years meat is one of the most expensive items on the shopping list.

Most of us tend to play safe. We buy what we know will please the family, choice roasting joints and chops or steaks which are easy to grill or fry successfully. So this kind of meat becomes more and more costly, while the many cheap cuts which are just as delicious and nourishing but require more careful cooking are almost a dead loss to the butcher. Many are no longer stocked at all, since there is so little demand for them, and go straight to the makers of pies and canned foods. As it is not yet possible, in spite of every scientific miracle, to breed animals which produce less offal and stewing meat, and more rib roasts, your butcher is bound to charge more for the favourite cuts. One result of this trend is that cheaper joints, such as silverside which were once considered only suitable for pot-roasting and boiling are now offered as prime roasting joints, and if they are not very carefully roasted they may be tough, dry and disappointing.

One of the best ways I know of saving money on food bills is to learn how to cook every variety and cut of meat to the best advantage. Then you can enjoy a superb fillet of veal, or sirloin of beef, for special occasions and yet provide a meal fit for the most discerning every day of the week from much less expensive cuts.

This book is intended to be an up-to-date guide to selecting meat and preparing it to suit today's style of living; cooking meat for and from the freezer; using an automatic oven and other gadgets such as a blender, or rotisserie if you have one. Many recipes are clearly illustrated with step by step photographs. Try your hand at making simple but delicious foreign dishes – curry, kebabs, risotto, even Chinese sweet-and-sour specialities – for entertaining, an elegant guard of honour or crown roast of lamb, and the famous fondue bourguignonne. To help you become more adventurous in using other cookery books I have included a comprehensive glossary of cookery terms which you may encounter, especially when reading about recipes from abroad. There are lists and line drawings to help you build up a useful *batterie de cuisine*, as the French call the kitchen cupboards and drawers stocked with pans and utensils, to help you attack meat cookery!

To avoid repetition, the basic methods of meat cookery are described at the beginning of the book so that you may refer to them when necessary; also given at the beginning are lists of herbs and spices used for flavouring and seasoning. To widen the scope of the book there is a section of marinades to choose from, all of which enhance the flavour and tenderise the texture of meat. There is a section devoted to stuffings which you may use as alternatives to those given in the recipes. Try an unusual one with pimentos and honey for instance. Details are given for the great basic sauces and soups of all kinds from hearty and economical ones to the most delicate consommé, to make use of the bones and trimmings.

Garnishes are pictured in line drawings to show you exactly how they should look and there is some down-to-earth advice on the appropriate wines to serve with various meat dishes.

With freezer owners in mind, I have dealt carefully with the problems of buying meat in bulk, having it cut up and wrapping it to pack away conveniently in a home freezer. All recipes especially suitable for freezing are marked thus * and freezing instructions are given.

Because an important part of your expertise as a meat cook is to make the best use of economical cuts, there is a big section of appetising recipes for everyday meals which give the best possible value for money. This section includes two suggestions for batch cooking from a bulk purchase to save you hours of work in the kitchen, and two complete meals for an automatic oven. To enable you to shop with confidence the recipes are preceded by hints on judging the quality of meat from each animal, recognising the different cuts and methods of carving.

Then there is another section of more exotic recipes for entertaining, ranging from an informal fondue party to an elegant dinner. Nevertheless, they are all so easy that none of them need frighten an inexperienced hostess.

Not every cook is catering for the needs of a large family and to relate the general information to special needs I have given a section to suit a person who lives alone but enjoys varied and appetising meals, and another for couples who cannot take advantage of recipes which involve cooking in quantity. Last but not least I have remembered the problems of the invalid who needs especially tempting and delicious food, but whose diet has to be strictly limited.

Since we are great meat eaters in this country and meat is the centrepiece of so many meals, I hope this book will help you to become an expert on meat cookery and put you well on the way to winning your Cordon Bleu.

Audrey Ellis

Useful facts and figures

I have worked out a plan for converting recipes from British measures to their approximate metric equivalents. For ease of measuring it is recommended that solids and liquids be taken to the nearest number of grammes and millilitres which is divisible by 25.

If the nearest unit of 25 gives scant measure, the liquid content in a recipe must also be reduced. For example, by looking at the chart below you will see that 1 oz. is 28 g. to the nearest whole figure but it is only 25 g. when rounded off.

Ounces	Approx. g. and ml. to the nearest whole figure	Approx. to nearest unit of 25	Ounces	Approx. g. and ml. to the nearest whole figure	Approx. to nearest unit of 25
1	28	25	11	311	300
2	57	50	12	340	350
3	85	75	13	368	375
4	113	125	14	396	400
5	142	150	15	428	425
6	170	175	16	456	450
7	198	200	17	484	475
8	226	225	18	522	500
9	255	250	19	541	550
10	283	275	20	569	575

Note: When converting quantities over 20 oz. first add the appropriate figures in the column giving the nearest whole number of grammes, *not* those given to the nearest unit of 25, then adjust to the nearest unit of 25.

LIQUID MEASURES

6 tablespoons (4 fl. oz.)	125 ml.
8 tablespoons (5 fl. oz. or ¼ pint)	150 ml.
½ pint (10 fl. oz.)	275 ml.
¾ pint (15 fl. oz.)	425 ml.
1 pint (20 fl. oz.)	575 ml.

OVEN TEMPERATURE CHART

	°F	°C	Gas Mark
Very cool	225	110	¼
	250	130	½
Cool	275	140	1
	300	150	2
Moderate	325	170	3
	350	180	4
Moderately hot	375	190	5
	400	200	6
Hot	425	220	7
	450	230	8
Very hot	475	240	9

The Celsius (formerly Centigrade) equivalents are the temperatures recommended by The Electricity Council.

Notes for American users

The American edition of this book shows the U.S. cuts of veal, beef, lamb and pork and the chapters on these meats have also been Americanized. For cuts of meat mentioned elsewhere in the book consult the following list.

Each recipe has an American column giving U.S. cup measures for the ingredients.
The following list gives American equivalents or substitutes for some terms used in the book.

British	American
Pudding basin	Pudding mold/ovenproof bowl
Mixer/liquidiser	Mixer/blender
Pie dish	Pie pan
Kitchen paper	Paper towels
Cocktail stick	Wooden toothpick
Frying pan	Skillet
Grill	Broil/broiler
Greaseproof paper	Wax paper
Kitchen foil	Aluminum foil
Piping bag	Pastry bag
Piping tube	Nozzle/tip
Veal	
Escalopes	Scallops
Beef	
Topside	Rolled rump
Fillet	Tenderloin
Silverside (fresh or salted)	Fresh brisket or corned beef
Fore rib	Standing rib roast
Brisket	Fresh brisket
Skirt	Flank
Leg	Heel of round
Lamb	
Best end of neck	Rack of lamb
Pork	
Leg	Fresh ham
Hand and spring	Fresh picnic shoulder
Belly	Flank

Note: The British pint measures 20 fluid ounces whereas the American pint equals 16 fluid ounces.

Glossary of terms

Angostura bitters An aromatic preparation made to the same secret recipe since 1824; it was made originally in Venezuela and is a combination of vegetable and spice extracts and adds a distinctive aromatic flavour to soups, casseroles, sauces, salads and marinades.

Aspic A clear jelly used to cover and decorate any meat, game, poultry or vegetable and to make hors d'oeuvres. Also called calves' foot jelly. The commercially produced powder form of aspic is made from extracts of bones of meat, fish or poultry.

Bain-marie A French utensil to help keep foods, often liquids, simmering without boiling. It is a type of double saucepan with the food in the top portion being kept hot over boiling water. It can also be a shallow pan of water in which is placed another vessel containing food to be baked in the oven.

Barbecue To barbecue originally meant to cook a whole carcass on a spit over an open fire. Nowadays smaller portions of meat are cooked in this way on a grid on kebab skewers over hot embers. The food is usually basted with a highly seasoned sauce. Meat has a very characteristic flavour when cooked in this way.

Bard To cover lean cuts of meat or game with thin strips of pork fat or streaky bacon before roasting or braising in the oven. This helps to keep the meat moist during cooking.

Baste To spoon or pour fat, juices or sauce over meats while cooking in the oven or under the grill, to keep them moist and add flavour at the same time.

Beurre manié A mixture of equal quantities of butter and plain flour kneaded together to a paste. This is then added in small pieces to a stew, casserole or sauce to thicken it.

Blanch To preheat, but not cook, in boiling water or steam. This helps to loosen skins of some fruits, vegetables or nuts, to remove excess salt or bitterness from some vegetables and bacon or ham, and to prepare fruits and vegetables for freezing or preserving processes.

Bouillon A clear broth, soup or stock made from boiling beef, veal or poultry with vegetables in water, to give a well-flavoured liquid; it is strained before using.

Bouquet garni A bunch or muslin bag of herbs, selected by the cook according to the dish being prepared. This is removed before serving.

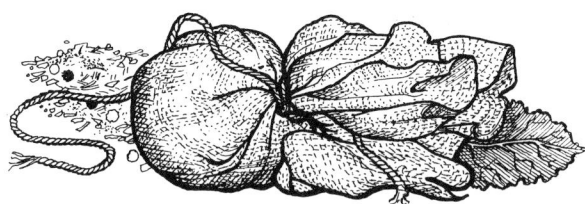

Brine A strong solution of kitchen salt or Mediterranean sea salt and water used to preserve meat and fish and for preparing vegetables for pickling.

Brochette A small skewer made of metal or more usually wood, used to hold small items of food for grilling or barbecuing or to keep meat in shape while cooking.

Broiling The American term for grilling.

Capers Cultivated in the Mediterranean countries they are the opened flower buds of the plant; used in caper and tartare sauce and for garnishing.

Cassoulet A dish originating from the Languedoc region of France, consisting of goose or duck with haricot beans, cooked together in a hot-pot. Pork or mutton can be used.

Charcuterie A shop where cold meats, sausage, brawn, galantines and pâtés etc. are sold. The term really applies to pork butchery and is the art of preparing meat for special methods of cookery.

Chine To cut through the backbone (end bone on the ribs or loin) so that chops or cutlets of lamb, veal or pork can be easily separated when carving.

Clarify To clear stock, broth or consommé by adding a slightly beaten egg white and crushed egg shell. The liquid is brought to the boil and any scum removed, then it is strained before using.

Fat is clarified by adding about one third the amount of water and heating until the water has evaporated. The fat is then strained and left to become cold, when the fat can be lifted off, and the impurities scraped from the underside. Butter is clarified by gentle heating so that the clear butter can be poured off.

Concasser A term most usually applied to tomatoes which are skinned, de-seeded and chopped.

Court-bouillon A stock in which other foods are cooked to add to their flavour. Basic ingredients could include stock, wine, vinegar, oil, onions, shallots or garlic, carrots, bay leaf, peppercorns and other herbs.

Croûtons Bread, trimmed and cut into various shapes and sizes before being sautéed in oil and butter. Used for garnishing.

Curing A process by which meat is preserved by dry salting or soaking in brine, sometimes followed by smoking.

Daube A method of cooking beef by braising in red wine and herbs; gives its name to the French daubière, the cooking pot used for the dish.

Demi-glace The name of a brown sauce, reduced and used to coat food to give a glazed appearance; can be flavoured with Madeira or sherry.

Devilled A method of cooking small pieces of meat, eggs and vegetables, which are sometimes marinated in a hot spicy piquant sauce before cooking with the sauce. Often curry powder is a main flavouring ingredient.

Faggot The term used to describe a tied bundle of herbs, similar to a bouquet garni; or a type of sausage (see page 48).

Fines herbes A mixture of several fresh herbs, the most important two being parsley and chervil; sometimes sage, thyme or tarragon are added.

Fricassée A traditional French stew of veal, chicken or lamb. The meat is cooked with vegetables in a white stock then thickened with cream and sometimes with egg yolks.

Gratin Or au gratin means to brown food in the oven or under a grill, usually coated with a white or cheese sauce, sprinkled with breadcrumbs and grated cheese, which gives a crisp golden finish.

Hanging Meat and game should always be well hung from a hook in a cold, dry, well-ventilated place, to tenderise the meat and help mature the flavour.

Julienne Usually vegetables, cut into thin matchstick-length pieces; can be used for garnishing meat dishes such as grilled steak.

Lard Cooking fat produced from melted down pork fat. To lard means to thread thin strips of pork fat or bacon through joints of meat with a special larding needle, to give flavour and moisture to the meat. Lardoons are the strips of pork fat or bacon used for threading through the meat.

Basic methods of meat cookery

Marinade A flavoured liquid in which meat is soaked and then subsequently cooked in or basted with to flavour and soften the meat fibres and to tenderise tougher cuts. Ingredients include red or white wine or wine vinegar, olive oil, carrots, onion, garlic and various herbs and spices.

Mirepoix A bed of mixed vegetables on which cuts of meat and poultry are braised; includes carrots, onion and celery, finely chopped and sautéed.

Papillote To cook *en papillote* means to enclose food in an oiled paper case before cooking in the oven.

Pot-au-feu A famous French dish of beef and vegetables cooked in a deep casserole or marmite also called the pot-au-feu.

Réchauffé The name given to cooked food when it is reheated; the food is sometimes adapted to form a different dish from the original.

Reduce To cook a liquid or sauce over high heat at a full boil to evaporate and reduce by the desired quantity. This helps improve flavour and consistency and thus the appearance.

Roux The basic mixture of equal quantities of melted butter and flour to which milk, water or stock is added to make a sauce or gravy, of varying consistency depending on the finished dish.

Sauté To cook food lightly turning it frequently in small amounts of oil or butter to seal the outside of meats, etc.

Sear or seal To seal the outside surface of meat, quickly in a very little fat to prevent the juices escaping during longer cooking.

Simmer To cook food well below boiling point, only an occasional bubble should rise to the surface. Temperature is about 185°F (85°C).

Tournedos A round steak of beef, cut about 1–1½ inches thick from the best part of the fillet.

Worcestershire sauce A commercially produced, highly seasoned, piquant sauce based on soy.

Zest The finely grated rind of an orange or lemon, not including the white pith.

Roasting

Quick roasting Roasting at high heat throughout cooking time, or for the first half hour to seal the meat and keep in the juices, then the heat is reduced for the remaining time. Suitable for prime joints. Basting is advisable with this method.

Slow roasting Roasting from a cold start in the oven, or at a relatively low temperature throughout cooking time, suitable for medium quality joints. A covered roasting tin with dimpled lid can be used, to keep very lean joints moist, or the joint can be lightly covered with foil, just crimped at the four corners to form a dome.

Note: At the end of this section there is a table for roasting meat straight from the freezer, in the frozen state.

Braising

The meat is first seared on all sides to retain the juice, then simmered in a small quantity of rich sauce in a covered vessel (either in the oven or on top of the cooker) often with vegetables which release more liquid during cooking to keep the meat moist. Suitable for medium quality cuts.

Pot-roasting

The meat is cooked slowly in a covered pan on top of the cooker, and is an alternative method to braising where the oven is not available, or a finish more comparable to a roast joint is required. The meat is first seared, in fat, then the pan covered and the meat cooked in the remaining fat and its own steam. The base of the pan must be heavy or the meat placed on a trivet. A little water can also be added to bring the liquid in the pan up to half an inch. The lid can be removed for the last half hour of cooking to let the joint brown.

Boiling

The method resembles stewing but is used more for large joints, such as leg of lamb or mutton, and ham or bacon joints. The meat is covered with cold water, brought to the boil, and then simmered, with the lid on the pan until the joint is tender. For salted meats, the water can be thrown away when it comes to the boil, and the process repeated with fresh water, to remove surplus salt. If somewhat flavourless, stock can be used instead of water.

Stewing
The favourite method for cooking coarse cuts of meat to tenderise them. The meat is sliced or cut into dice, lightly fried in fat with vegetables and other ingredients, then liquid is added and the vessel covered. It is simmered on top of the cooker at low heat until meat is tender. Sometimes ingredients which would be overcooked by this time are added towards the end of cooking time.

Casseroling
Virtually the same method as for stewing, but generally directions are to place the covered vessel in the oven. The meat and vegetables may be sautéed on top of the cooker first, to conserve the juices, but if the meat is well flavoured this step may be omitted in which case the gravy will be richer.

Grilling
The meat is exposed to direct heat under a hot grill, and turned part way through the cooking time. Only thin prime cuts are suitable, such as rump steak, lamb loin chops. The meat should be brushed with melted fat or oil, placed on greased grill bars if likely to stick, and turned to seal both sides before the full cooking time is allowed on the first side, otherwise juices may drip through into the grill pan and the meat become dry in cooking. Allow 4–7 minutes on each side according to the thickness of the cut.

Frying
Shallow frying An alternative to grilling for similar cuts, and for offal such as liver which tends to curl up on the grill grid. The meat is sealed in very shallow hot fat, the heat lowered and the cooking finished on both sides to the degree desired. Sausages should be fried slowly, and not pricked beforehand. Time as for grilling.
Deep frying Only suitable for croquettes, meat balls, and other made-up meat dishes where the meat requires little cooking and will cook more evenly if surrounded by the source of heat.

Storing raw and cooked meat
Prior to cooking, meat should be stored in a cool place, preferably in the refrigerator, or the old-fashioned larder, as it is highly perishable. Remove wrappings, wipe with a clean cloth, place on a dish and cover lightly with a muslin meat shade. Put on the larder shelf or, if you have to keep a large joint, wrap it in stockinette and hang up on a hook to allow air to circulate around the meat. To store in the refrigerator, the meat must be covered to prevent transference of cross flavours or aromas from other uncovered food in the cabinet. The more cut surfaces are exposed the quicker the meat will deteriorate, so mince, offal or diced meat should not be kept for more than 24 hours uncooked, or 2 days cooked in the larder. The colder temperature inside the refrigerator should make it possible to keep uncooked meat for up to 3 days and cooked meat up to 5 days. In a hot weather emergency, store uncooked meat in a marinade (see page 70).

Meat roasting chart

Beef

Quick	400°F, 200°C, Gas Mark 6	*Top grade joints* 20 minutes per lb. under done plus 20 minutes over for well done.
Slow	300°F, 150°C, Gas Mark 2	*Medium grade joints* 60 minutes for first lb. plus 20 minutes for each extra lb. under-done, 25 minutes, well done.

Veal

Quick	400°F, 200°C, Gas Mark 6	*Top grade joints* 30 minutes per lb. plus 30 minutes over. (Plus 15 minutes if covered.)
Slow	300°F, 150°C, Gas Mark 2	*Medium grade joints* 60 minutes for first lb. plus 25 minutes for each extra lb.

Lamb/mutton

400°F, 200°C, Gas Mark 6 reduce to 350°F, 180°C, Gas Mark 4, after 30 minutes.	20 minutes per lb. plus 20 minutes over.

Pork

400°F, 200°C, Gas Mark 6 reduce to 350°F, 180°C, Gas Mark 4, after 30 minutes.	30 minutes per lb. plus 30 minutes over.

Note: When roasting in a rotisserie, allow 15–30 minutes less cooking time.

Roasting chart for meat from the frozen state

Generally speaking small joints require to be cooked by the same calculation of one hour per pound as do large joints. This assumes that a satisfactory joint for roasting is taken to be one which weighs at least 2½ lb. and may weigh as much as 8 lb. The average family Sunday roast weighing 3–4 lb. poses no problems as far as timing is concerned, but a very large joint might only be suitable to serve for an evening meal.

If stuffing is to be served, cook this in a separate well-greased pan or form it into balls with floured hands and allow to cook for the necessary time, in the pan with the joint.

Beef *Prime roasting cuts such as sirloin, topside, etc.*
Weigh joint. Preheat oven to 400°F, 200°C, Gas Mark 6, place joint in roasting pan uncovered, for 10 minutes, to seal the meat. Cover with a sheet of foil, crimped at four corners so that the meat is partially but not completely protected from direct contact with oven heat. Reduce temperature to 350°F, 180°C, Gas Mark 4, and allow one hour per pound roasting time from this point. If meat is preferred rare, remove foil and insert meat thermometer to approximately the centre of the joint, 40 minutes before cooking time expires. Check from then onwards every 10 minutes until thermometer indicates temperature required: rare – 140°F (60°C), medium – 155°F (68°C), well done – 170°F (76°C).

Fillet Weigh joint. Seal in preheated oven as for other prime cuts of beef. This is the only joint which requires less than one hour per pound cooking time, even if preferred well done. Enclose completely in a parcel of foil and allow 45 minutes per pound. Open parcel (but do not remove foil) and insert meat thermometer 20 minutes before time expires. Leave foil folded back while cooking is completed and carry out checks as above.

Medium roasting cuts such as silverside, fore rib, etc.
Weigh joint. Preheat oven to 350°F, 180°C, Gas Mark 4, then either place joint in a roasting pan with a dimpled lid, or in a roasting bag, leaving sufficient room round the joint to accommodate its juices. Roast for one hour per pound. If a particularly well done or rare joint is required, a check can be made with the meat thermometer as above, either by inserting the thermometer in the meat and replacing the dimpled lid, or plunging it *through* the roasting bag into the joint, above the level of the juices. If the joint is very lean, a small amount of dripping should be added to the pan or bag.

Note: One hour per pound gives the medium to well done result, preferred by the majority for beef.

To make *Yorkshire pudding* to serve with roast beef, sieve 2 oz. plain flour (U.S. ½ cup all-purpose flour) with a pinch of salt. Add 1 egg and ¼ pint milk or milk and water (U.S. ⅔ cup) and mixing with a wooden spoon gradually draw in the flour from around the edges – work from the centre of the basin to the sides and mix to a smooth batter. Beat for 2–3 minutes, cover and leave to stand. Stir again before using. For individual Yorkshire puddings grease about eight bun tins and heat thoroughly in the oven, then pour a little of the batter into each. Bake in a hot oven, 425°F, 220°C, Gas Mark 7 for 12–15 minutes until crisp and golden.

Lamb *All joints suitable for roasting are prime cuts such as leg, shoulder, best end of neck, loin*
Weigh joint. Proceed as for beef, open roasting to seal the meat before enclosing it in a 'dome' of foil, or roast as for medium beef cuts in a dimpled roaster or roasting bag. The first method gives a crisp skin and a slightly pink tinge to the meat near the bone if you prefer lamb, as the French do, slightly rare. Cooking lamb from the frozen state for less than one hour per pound is not recommended. The meat thermometer, if used, should register 180°F (82°C).

Veal Follow same instructions as for lamb.

Pork *Roasting joints required with crackling, such as leg or hand and spring*
Weigh joint. Place in a preheated oven at 400°F, 200°C, Gas Mark 6, for 20 minutes before covering and reducing the heat to 350°F, 180°C, Gas Mark 4. This ensures a crisp crackling. Calculate cooking time from this point, allowing one hour per pound and cover with a 'dome' of foil. As pork should not be eaten even slightly under done, this length of cooking time is always required. For very large joints, it is really advisable to use a meat thermometer. Pork is not fully cooked until it reaches a temperature of 190°F (88°C).

Joints from which skin has been removed
Weigh joint, proceed as above, reducing period of cooking in a moderately hot oven from 20 minutes to 10 minutes.

Herb and spice seasoning guide

The use of herbs enhances the flavour of many meat dishes. They can add just a hint of tangy sweetness, as do the delicately scented aromatic sweet herbs, or a more robust touch as do chives, garlic and horseradish. Fresh herbs are used in much larger quantities than dried herbs, so do not be surprised if a recipe calls for a tablespoon or more of freshly chopped parsley but indicates only a half teaspoon of dried basil or thyme. The following herbs are those most often used in meat cookery.

Herbs quickly lose their flavour once picked, unless kept with the stems in water, so it is a good rule to buy little and often, or pick only what is immediately required from the garden. Dried herbs must be kept in an airtight container or they become musty and flavourless.

Basil This has a slightly peppery clove-like taste, is popular in Italian style stews which include tomato and goes well with beef or veal.

Bay leaves Use these in a bouquet garni, as a flavouring for stock, marinades and sauces. Remove from the dish before serving. A branch of bay leaves can be hung up in the kitchen and retains its flavour longer than herbs which wither when cut. Very good with beef and pork.

Chives Have a more delicate flavour than onion and grow freely even in a window-sill pot almost all the year round. The long narrow leaves are chopped finely and used to garnish meat salads, or for any other purpose where a mild onion flavour is desired. The flower heads should be picked off as they form to keep the plant producing leaves.

Dill Has a sweetish flavour like aniseed, and is best with delicate white meats, such as lamb and pork. The fresh herb has feathery frond-like leaves, is sometimes called *dill weed*. Dill seed is used in curries and stews.

Garlic Most pungent of all herbs, and imparts its strong onion flavour to everything the cut clove touches. Each tiny clove, when peeled and crushed, can flavour a saucepanful of stew, two at the most are recommended except for Mediterranean and oriental dishes. Particularly delicious with lamb and beef dishes. For the timid, it is sometimes enough to rub the pan or serving dish with half a cut clove. (To crush, use a garlic press or the flat blade of a knife plus a little salt; wash all utensils used for preparation well.) The bulb or root, not the leaves, is used in cooking.

Horseradish Has a very strong flavour reminiscent of mustard. The root is peeled, grated, and often blended with cream, grated apple or cooked beetroot to make a mild sauce. This is served with beef.

Lovage The plant looks like celery in miniature and the stems are used to give a celery flavour to stews. The leaves and seed can also be used, but it is very strong and if not used sparingly, may taste bitter.

Marjoram A versatile herb with round, dark green leaves and mauve flowers, which has a spicy, sweetish flavour, and goes very well with all meats. The leaves are a favourite ingredient where mixed herbs are called for. It should be picked and dried before flowering, as the leaves taste bitter once the flowers form.

Mint There are many varieties of mint, with widely differing flavours. It grows freely, like a weed when once established, and is difficult to control. Goes well with lamb. The most common varieties, spearmint, apple mint, peppermint and eau de cologne mint all have recognisable flavours. The leaves only are used in meat dishes, the whole stem used when boiling potatoes, but is removed before serving.

Oregano Has the same flavour as marjoram, but stronger. The leaves are used for many Italian dishes, and especially with beef.

Parsley The most versatile of herbs; used chopped for flavouring and as a garnish in the form of sprigs. The stalks are used to flavour stock and stews; the curly leaves in sauces, mixed with other herbs, in stews with all kinds of meat. Parsley sauce is served with boiled mutton or baked meat loaves.

Rosemary The small spiky leaves are often too hard to chop, and must be left whole. A sprig of rosemary added to the roasting pan can be used to flavour a joint, or put in a stew, and discarded when the meat is cooked. Very good with lamb.

Sage The leaves, greyish green in colour, have a strong distinctive flavour, very popular with pork, in stuffings, or in pie fillings which include pork.

Savory A rather unusual herb, which is used in the

form of sprigs for boiling with vegetables (as with mint) but the leaves only in stews, especially with pork or veal.

Tarragon Although slightly bitter, the flavour is reminiscent of liquorice. It goes well with most offal, especially kidneys, and sweetbreads, but only a pinch of the chopped leaves is required.

Thyme Ordinary thyme is strongly flavoured; used in sprigs as part of a bouquet garni for all meat dishes. Lemon thyme is far more delicate, particularly good with lamb.

Spices

The use of spices has, since ancient times, served the dual purpose of flavouring and preserving meat and in pre-refrigeration days of masking the fact that meat was 'high'. Most are strongly flavoured, and used sparingly. The following are those most cooks keep in stock for meat cookery.

Allspice The whole berries, tied in muslin like a bouquet garni add piquancy to stews and stock, or meat soups. Remove before serving.

Caraway The flavour of the seeds is sweet but like liquorice; can be added to dumplings to serve with a goulash, to cabbage to serve with lamb, or any highly seasoned stew.

Cardamom The whole seeds are useful for curries as they have a sweet yet pungent flavour. For sweet dishes they are used ground.

Cayenne Also used in curries; this hottest of all peppers is an ingredient of curry powder but can be used sparingly, alone, in devilled dishes.

Chilli powder Ground from small red chilli peppers, this is hotter and more peppery than the American chili powder, which blends other milder spices with it. It is noticeably less strong than cayenne.

Cinnamon The sticks are more used to flavour sweet dishes, but a pinch of ground cinnamon improves curries and adds interest to a spiced marinade.

Cloves Have an extremely sharp, yet sweet, flavour and two or three are often stuck into an onion to flavour a stew; or they are added directly to beef stews, along with bay leaves, as in a bouquet garni.

Coriander A mild, fruity-flavoured spice. The seeds are used whole in curries, or ground in curry powder, added to pork or lamb stews, or to tomato sauce to serve with beef.

Cumin A stronger flavour than coriander, but the seeds are used in the same way.

Curry power A small pinch enlivens réchauffées, meat cakes and loaves and all types of made-up dishes. It is a blend of spices, some sweet and some hot; a typical blend includes turmeric, cardamom, coriander, cumin and mustard seed, dried chillies, cayenne, ginger, cinnamon, mace and cloves.

Ginger This is a very hot spice, used in marinades, in the form of whole pieces of the root, or ground in stews and basting sauces. Very good with pork and beef.

Juniper berries Have a strong rather bitter flavour, much favoured in Mediterranean dishes, with veal and pork, and in pâtés.

Mace Strong, more bitter flavour than nutmeg, but used in the same way in the form of blades (now not easy to obtain) or powdered, with veal and pork.

Mustard Strong, pungent spice with characteristic yellow colour, used ground as a powder, or made up with water or vinegar in devilled meat dishes or any that need hot flavouring. Continental mustards are milder and darker in colour than English. Remember you need less mustard powder than made mustard.

Nutmeg An aromatic spice not used much in meat dishes but with accompaniments, such as creamed potatoes, carrots or spinach.

Paprika pepper Has the same characteristic red colour but is much milder and sweeter than cayenne; comes from another species of the capsicum family, and is favoured in eastern European meat cookery, particularly in goulashes.

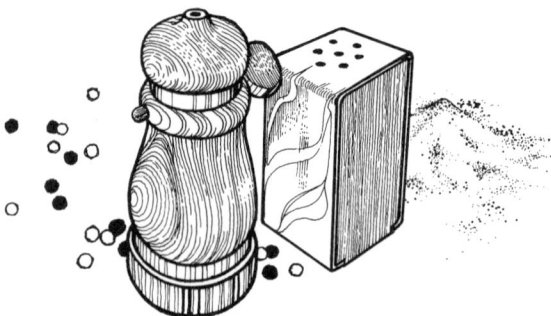

Pepper Black is far more pungent than white pepper. Use white for delicately flavoured and lightly coloured dishes, and with all white meats. Whole peppercorns are often recommended in old recipes, especially for beef and mutton, and as part of a bouquet garni.

Saffron Flavours pleasantly and colours yellow at the same time; used in curries and for tinting rice to serve with meat dishes. Use the dried petals (a sort of crocus) or in ground form.

Turmeric Delicate, yellow spice used ground for curries and middle eastern meat dishes, especially with lamb and mutton.

Note: Salt, which is a mineral not a spice, is the ingredient most often used to flavour meat and in larger quantities to preserve it. Seasoned salts are useful aids – such as celery salt, onion salt, garlic salt and hickory smoked salt.

Utensils

You may not be able to invest in the whole range of equipment listed below immediately, but you will find it easier to become an expert meat cook if you have the right tools for the job. In the case of some items, it really does pay to buy the best you can afford; as in the case of knives which ought to be so sharp they need using with care. Keep these on a magnetic wall rack or in a special knife compartment in a drawer as the fine edge is often damaged if knives are jumbled up with other cooking utensils.

Useful basic equipment

Knives
meat chopper (optional)
chopping knife
boning knife
vegetable knife
small serrated knife
carving knife (with comfortable grip)
ham carving knife (thin flexible blade)
matching carving fork (with guard)
knife sharpener or steel
palette knife
cannel knife (or *decorateur*)
meat slice
slotted serving slice

Forks
table fork
3-pronged cooking fork

Spoons
basting spoon
slotted draining spoon
ladle
1 large wooden spoon
1 small wooden spoon

Other items
pudding basins, 1½- and 2-pint size
pie dishes, 2- and 2½-pint size
large round strainer
conical gravy strainer
small nylon sieve

colander
kitchen scales
heat-resistant measuring jugs, ½- and 1-pint size
set of British standard measuring spoons
steamer to fit saucepan
frying basket to fit saucepan
grater
mincer
large wooden chopping board
small wooden chopping board
flour dredger
wooden skewers
metal skewers, large and small
larding and trussing needles
thin twine
wooden cocktail sticks
roasting pan with dimpled lid
Yorkshire pudding tin
pastry brush
kitchen scissors
meat roasting thermometer
meat tenderiser
trivet
garlic press
wire whisk
cork-screw
potato peeler
paper kitchen towels
can opener
kitchen foil
rolling pin
meat bat or mallet
set of 3 mixing bowls
potato scoop
potato masher

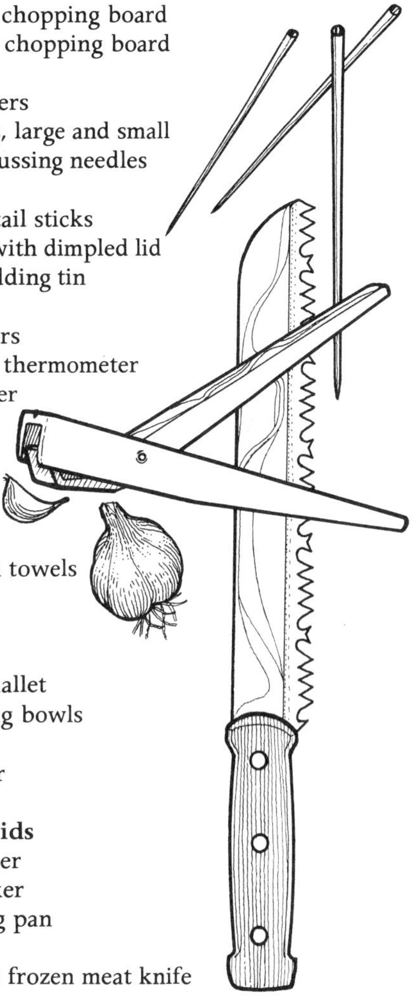

Additional aids
electric blender
pressure cooker
electric frying pan
rotisserie
double-edged frozen meat knife

Pans and casseroles

Good holloware is often expensive. You may have to begin with a small selection, but try to build up a collection of durable pans and casseroles which, with care, will last the average cook's lifetime.

Your major investment is bound to be a good set of saucepans. When choosing, check that each pan is well balanced, stands securely even if empty, lid fits tightly, base is thick enough to prevent thickened stews from burning, interior surface is damage resistant and easy to clean, knobs and handles are properly insulated. Larger pans have a pan grip opposite the handle for easy lifting.

Casseroles which can also be used in the oven are particularly useful but check that handles and grips are ovenproof too.

Choose from the following materials
Enamelled cast iron Sturdy but heavy to handle. Can be obtained with non-stick surface.
Aluminium Light to handle, conducts heat well but needs careful cleaning or it tends to become pitted.
Stainless steel Medium weight, extremely durable, can be obtained with copper clad base for quick heat conduction.

Enamelled steel pans are often decorated with attractive designs.
Copper Medium to heavy weight, cooks evenly and conducts heat well, excellent for sauté pans.

Glass ceramic Requires careful cleaning but can be taken straight from refrigerator or freezer to oven heat.

In addition to the materials mentioned above, ovenproof casseroles are available in glazed and unglazed earthenware which is cheap but breaks rather easily, and ovenproof glass.

Recommended basic equipment
set of 4 saucepans with lids, $1\frac{1}{4}$-, 2-, 5- and 8-pint capacity
set of 3 casseroles with lids, 2-, $3\frac{1}{2}$- and 5-pint capacity
set of 3 gratin dishes
frying pans 1 large 9-inch, 1 small 6-inch
shallow sauté pan
shallow oval and round entrée dishes

Bulk buying for the freezer

If you have never previously bought meat wholesale, do shop around for competitive prices and services among the various possible purveyors of meat in bulk before placing a large order. To buy, for example, a hindquarter of beef which may weigh as much as 180 lb. and find that it has not been butchered or packed according to your family requirements would be a very expensive mistake. Here are my golden rules for buying meat in bulk.

1. Go for good quality meat, even if you pay a penny per pound more than the lowest price quoted. Insist on beef being properly hung before delivery or it may be tough. Inform the butcher if you like your beef particularly well hung (ten days rather than a week). Remember that although a hindquarter includes the choicest cuts it always weighs more than a forequarter (which is about 100 lb.). Because it weighs less, the forequarter is a more manageable choice but includes many cuts only suitable for stews and minced beef.

2. Especially with regard to beef, make a list of the cuts included in your order and note the purposes for which each cut can be used. Ask the butcher to advise you what proportion of meat you will receive that is suitable for roasting, braising and so on before you order. The first time, ask him to bag the meat in convenient quantities and mark each pack with a description of the cut and purpose for which it is best suited.

3. If you have a preference for meat sliced for braising, mention this and ask the butcher to do this job for you or he may dice it all, or worse still leave it in large pieces. If he advises mincing the coarser meat and you want to freeze it uncooked, ensure that he does not add too much of the waste fat as a high proportion of fat shortens the storage life. If you have a pan large enough, ask for all the bones and make stock with these. Surplus beef fat can be rendered down to make excellent dripping, but the butcher will probably not send you either the bones or the fat unless you specially ask for them. Persuade him to saw the bones up to fit into your largest saucepan! He may also be prepared to mince the suet for you which again saves time in your own kitchen.

Lamb When you first decide to buy meat in bulk for your freezer, it is easiest to start with a whole lamb. A small one will be lean and need weigh no more than 26–30 lb. The cuts are all well known and easily recognisable. The only special advice needed is to decide beforehand whether you wish the best end of neck left as a whole joint for roasting, divided into cutlets, or boned and divided into noisettes. There is not a large proportion of stewing meat and recipes are given here for using this in various ways.

Pork A whole pig represents a lot of meat but a half pig is also a good purchase for the beginner as it produces about 50 lb. of meat. Do not be surprised to find your purchase includes the head and trotters. The cuts are mainly for roasting and frying and the only ones likely to be unfamiliar are the belly and spare ribs. Since pork is a very fat meat, do not buy more than you can use up within six months.

Beef Because it is a larger animal, you cannot avoid buying a lot of meat unsuitable for roasting and frying. If, for example, your family will eat nothing but roasts and grills, you will have more of a problem than a bargain on your hands. You may also find yourself landed with far more unaccustomed cuts than you knew ever existed, such as the following: *brisket, silverside and thick flank* – suitable for very slow roasting, pot-roasting or braising; *chuck steak and skirt* – suitable for braising; *leg, shin and neck (or clod)* – suitable for stewing only. Skirt can be sliced thinly across the grain while still partially frozen and fried to make economical minute steaks.

Veal Your wholesale butcher may persuade you that half a calf is an economical purchase. Of all meat, I consider it the least satisfactory buy for the home freezer. The slight tenderising process of breaking down the fibres of the meat by freezing is not an advantage in the case of veal which is such a tender meat. The loss of flavour on the other hand, although not noticeable in more strongly flavoured meat, is just perceptible in veal which has an extremely delicate flavour in any case. If you do buy veal, ask your butcher to slice the escalopes very carefully and thinly and dice or chop all the coarser cuts suitable for stewing and braising, or using as pie veal, leaving you only the best joints for roasting.

Wrapping for freezer storage

Experienced freezer owners will know that it is necessary to protect meat with a moisture-vapour-proof wrapping material or container. As meat has a low water content, it is not necessary to leave a headspace for the expansion of water on freezing. In fact it is best to wrap meat as closely as possible to exclude the danger of oxidation or 'freezer burn' by exposure of the surface of the meat to the excessively cold dry air of the freezer cabinet or indeed within the pack itself. Sharp bones should be protected by pads of foil to prevent them from piercing the wrap or pack, or damaging other items in the freezer. Nothing is more annoying than finding a number of small cuts inextricably frozen together when you wish to remove a few items from a large bag. All small cuts which may require dividing before cooking (and this does not refer to stewing pieces) should be separated by dividers of kitchen foil or sheet polythene within the pack. Also, seal packs which contain the number of portions usually required by your family for the meal, such as sets of six chops to serve a family of three. Strong stock, well reduced, made from the bones, can be stored in tumbler type containers, ice-cube trays, or gusseted bags placed in a box-shaped container as a liner until the liquid content is fully frozen. Cooked casserole dishes can be conveniently frozen in freezer-foil liners inside your favourite casserole or a saucepan of handy size. They will then fit exactly into the vessel to be used for reheating, with the foil removed.

Defrosting tips

Chops, steaks, sausages and thin cuts of meat such as escalopes may be cooked from the frozen state quite easily if properly packed with foil dividers to enable you to separate them. It is also possible to roast a frozen joint if the instructions on page 10 are carefully followed.

If, however, there is sufficient time, and you prefer to allow meat to thaw out before cooking, do this if possible in the refrigerator.

It takes approximately four to six times longer for meat to defrost completely in a refrigerator than at room temperature, but the slower thawing period does allow the meat to re-absorb the juices which may be lost if the meat is thawed out too quickly.

Pork should always be defrosted in the refrigerator because of the special risk of contamination if allowed to defrost at room temperature. Other meats can be thawed at room temperature if space in the refrigerator is limited or time is short.

Beef and lamb can be left in their freezer wrappings, as they tend to drip during the defrosting process. Veal should be unwrapped and just protected with a loose covering of muslin or a wire mesh shade. Casseroles and braised dishes can be placed in a pre-heated oven, in the frozen state, to defrost and reheat, or they can be allowed to defrost in the refrigerator overnight, still covered.

Meat should be used as soon as possible after thawing and should be kept in the refrigerator. Meat which has a great many cut surfaces open to the air, such as minced meat, should be used within 24 hours of defrosting. Larger cuts and joints can be stored in the coldest part of the refrigerator for a few days but defrosted meat is very perishable and should be cooked well within a week.

Storage time-table for frozen meat

Surplus fat should be trimmed from meat for freezing as fat goes rancid and shortens the storage life of the lean meat. The temperature inside the freezer cabinet must never rise above $0°F (-18°C)$ during storage.

Stuffing, because of the seasonings and herbs used, and because it is usually based on breadcrumbs, also shortens the period during which meat can be safely stored.

Type of meat	Months
Veal, escalopes, chops	3–4
Veal, roasts	4–8
Beef	8–12
Lamb, chops	3–4
Lamb, roasts	8–12
Pork, chops	3–4
Pork, roasts	4–8
Minced meat	2–3
Offal	3–4
Cooked meats and casseroles etc.	3–4
Stuffed joints	1–3
Sausages, seasoned	1
Sausages, unseasoned	6

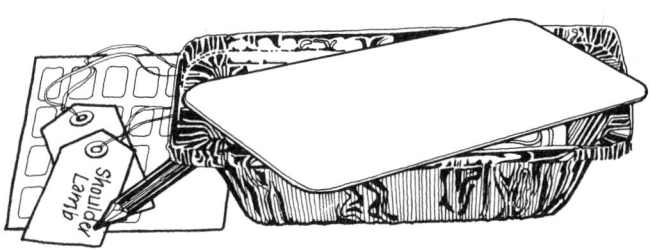

Veal

Veal is meat from calves of either sex. The best veal comes usually from milk-fed animals between six and ten weeks of age and weighing about 150 lb. The young of beef cattle are divided into two groups: vealers, usually less than three months old and weighing from 110–180 lb.; and calves from three to nine months old and weighing up to 300 lb. which produce slightly more mature meat.

Veal is expensive because it does not keep well and tends to spoil a few days after the animal is slaughtered, instead of maturing as beef does. It is rather a dry meat because the calf has not had time to acquire fat and since the natural flavor is not strong it needs very careful choice of seasonings and other flavors when used for casserole or braised dishes.

HOW TO CHOOSE VEAL

The flesh should be pale pink. The more mature the animal and the more it has subsisted on feed other than milk, the more red the lean will be. Although it is always soft it should not be either flabby or extremely moist. The internal fat should be firm and very white. Fat which comes from parts near the skin may vary from pinkish to creamy white. Veal bones are almost translucent compared with bones from older animals. When fresh they are white tinged with pink and produce a good setting stock although it has little flavor.

Do not buy veal which is noticeably yellowish or has a dry brownish skin. Unless the color looks really fresh and appetizing, the cooked meat may be tainted with a distinctly off flavor although it may still be safe to eat. There is, however, no reason to mistrust veal with skin which looks blistered. This is merely the result of the way the veal has been dressed, which forces air under the skin.

VARIETY MEATS

The calf provides some of the most tender and delicious variety meats which have the added advantage of being very quick to cook.

Brains These are usually poached in a white stock made from the bones of the animal and served with a lightly-flavored cream sauce. They can also be fried. They are bought by the set and two sets are sufficient to serve three or four as an entrée dish.

Feet Like the head, they can be used to make brawn or aspic or for any dishes which are required to set firmly, such as the filling of a pie. It is usual to add meat from other parts of the animal as there is little meat on the feet and it is extremely gelatinous.

Head Today this is usually served only as a brawn. Few modern housewives will even possess a pan large enough to cook a whole head. Ask the butcher to divide it into four parts and if possible to bone it for you. It is usually cooked with the tongue and brains if required for brawn, but both brains and tongue are also sold separately.

Heart Two veal hearts equal one beef heart. The veal heart is a little more tender but preparation is the same; allow $2\frac{1}{2}$–3 hours cooking time.

Kidneys These are not quite as tender as lamb kidneys but are suitable for broiling or sautéing. They are used like beef kidneys but each one is sufficient to serve two people.

Liver This very tender liver is ideal for sautéing or broiling and is delicious when served while still slightly pink in the center. It should be sliced very thinly.

Sweetbreads These are sold by the pair, which is sufficient to serve one person.

Tongue As the tongues are very small, it is usual to buy two or three, cook them and use to fill a medium-sized mold. Jellied stock is poured in to fill the mold level and when set the tongues are turned out and sliced across for serving.

All variety meats from the calf must be extremely fresh and as they spoil quickly make sure that any you are offered at a bargain price look light in color and are fairly moist.

VARIOUS USES FOR CUTS OF VEAL

There are a number of bony cuts which can be roasted but are better boned, stuffed, and tied or skewered to make a well-shaped roasting joint. These cuts include the leg, shoulder, shank, and breast. Chops and cutlets or round steak from the top of the leg are all suitable for broiling and panfrying but tend to shrink very much if cooked quickly on a high heat. For dishes such as goulash, boneless breast, shoulder, or shank are used. The shank and breast are also useful to add to the head or foot for a galantine.

Veal stew meat, an economical cut, usually consists mainly of finely diced shoulder and breast meat and trimmings. Any cut of veal is tender enough for a pot-roast or braised dish, the shoulder being most often used. The rib roast and loin roast are the prime cuts for roasting and really pay for the use of imagination in the choice of stuffing. The flavor of the stuffing impregnates and adds its own aroma to the unemphatic flavor of veal.

Veal scallops are small thin boneless slices usually from the leg. See page 50 for a recipe for escalopes de veau meunière and page 49 for stuffed and rolled roulades de veau. If the butcher does not have veal scallops you can make them yourself by pounding a thin veal cutlet with a mallet until it is very thin, and then cutting from this 4-inch round or oval pieces.

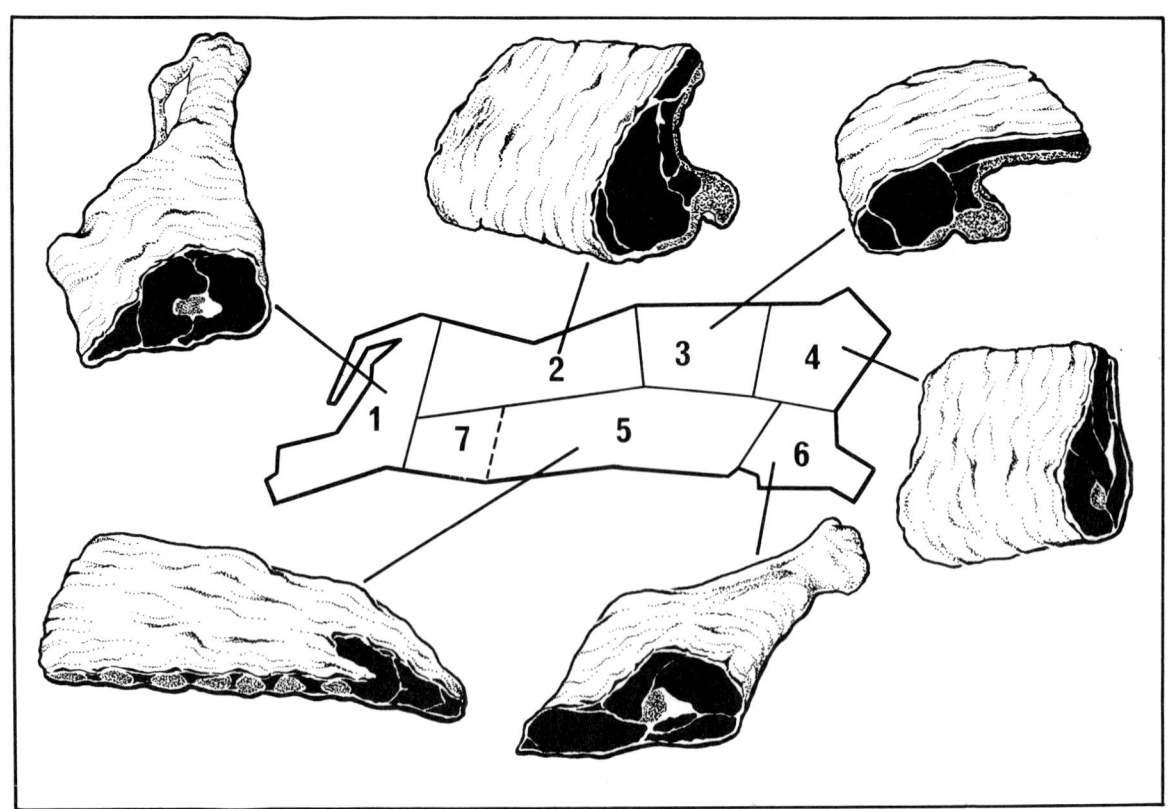

Cooking methods for cuts of veal

1 **Leg** Gives standing rump roast and rolled rump roast, shank half, and leg (round) center cut all suitable for roasting; heel of round and hind shank for braising, round steak (cutlet) for braising or panfrying.
2 **Loin** Gives loin chops, kidney chops, and sirloin steaks for braising or panfrying; sirloin roast and loin roast for braising or roasting.
3 **Rib** Gives rib roast and crown roast; rib chops for braising or panfrying.
4 **Shoulder** Gives blade roast and arm roast for roasting or braising; blade and arm steaks for braising or panfrying. Shoulder can also be boned and rolled for roasting or braising.
5 **Breast** Boned, stuffed, and rolled for roasting or braising. Gives riblets and stew meat for braising.
6 **Shank** Braising.
7 **Flank** (not shown) Can either be ground or used for veal stew meat.

Roulades de veau (see page 49)

How to carve cooked veal joints

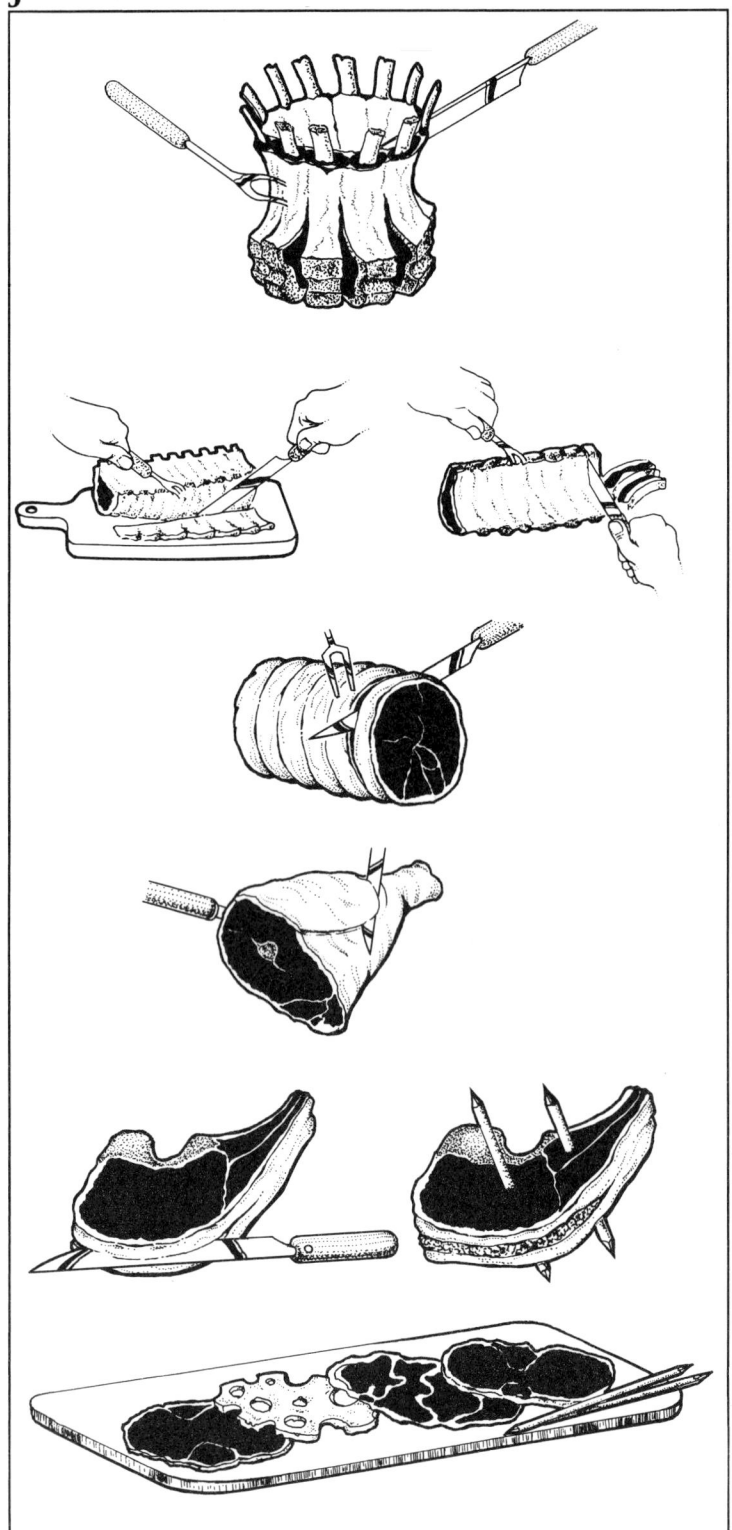

Crown roast Place the crown on the platter and hold it firmly with the fork. Slice down between the ribs, removing one rib chop at a time. The stuffing in the center of the crown, depending on its consistency, can either be sliced with the chop, served with a spoon, or sliced like a pie. Crown roasts can be made with either veal, lamb, or pork rib chops.

For carving a **loin roast** see instructions under pork (page 32).

For a **rolled roast** see instructions under lamb (page 28).

For carving a **veal shank half** cut horizontal slices down to the bone. Turn over joint and repeat on other side.

Preparing stuffed veal cuts
Pocket chops A thick veal chop can be sliced through with a sharp-pointed knife as far as the bone to make a pocket for stuffing. The stuffed chop must be secured with wooden toothpicks while panfrying; these are removed when serving.

Veal Cordon Bleu Two very thinly sliced veal scallops are sandwiched together with a slice of ham and a slice of Gruyère cheese. Secure with wooden toothpicks and if possible chill for an hour; remove toothpicks, coat with egg and soft bread crumbs and panfry.

Beef

All your expertise will be required in choosing good quality beef. There are so many different cuts, ranging from prime cuts for roasting, broiling, and panfrying, through the medium cuts which require slower cooking and are better braised or pot-roasted, to the coarse cuts for stews, goulash, pies, and puddings. Many of them look deceptively similar.

Beef is meat which comes from a mature animal and is more strongly flavored than veal. However, it may be tougher, especially in the coarser cuts, because it contains fully developed muscles, and sinews, especially in the meat of the flank or shank. High-grade beef usually comes from cattle weighing from 900–1300 lb. each, and the animals usually range from one to three years old. Regional preferences dictate what size carcass is shipped where. There is some variation in retail cuts across the country. For example you find that sirloin steaks are smaller in and around New York City as the sirloin section is divided into two pieces – the end nearest the flank is called the sirloin tip.

HOW TO CHOOSE BEEF

1 Meat of a bright red color, with a very slightly brownish tinge. If the lean has a dark, plum red appearance, it may have been exposed to the air for a considerable time, but it is also possible that it comes from an older animal.
2 The flesh should be firm without being dry and the lean should be flecked or marbled with fat, to keep the meat tender and moist in cooking.
3 The fat should be creamy white, ranging to a dark shade of cream according to the time of year and the source of the beef. Although extreme yellowness of the fat might indicate that you are being offered cow beef which would certainly be tough, it might be due to the breed of animal or the seasonal type of feed.
4 The amount of gristle should be very small in prime cuts; older animals, which produce tougher meat, will have a noticeable layer of gristle just under the outer layer of fat.
5 When you buy a joint for roasting, such as any boned and rolled joint, look at both ends. Extra fat is sometimes tucked into the middle of rolled joints.

Coarser cuts of meat are sometimes tenderized by machine and sold as minute steaks or Swiss steaks for panfrying, so make sure that if you intend to buy, for instance, sirloin steak, you do get what you ask for.

6 Beef which is a rather light color and appears to be dripping excessively, may not have been hung long enough. Beef in which the lean nearest the fat has a brownish tinge may have been hung too long. The length of hanging time before cooking (or packaging for freezing) is more important for beef than for any other meat.

VARIETY MEATS

Coming from a fully matured animal, these variety meats are richly flavored but inclined to be tough and require very long slow cooking.

Heart Because the beef heart is largely made up of strong muscle it is tough and dry unless filled with a moist stuffing and then slowly braised, or it can first be par-boiled, stuffed and then roasted. It should be first washed well in cold water. Either cover with foil or baste frequently. One heart with stuffing will serve six, but it can be bought sliced by the pound, for stewing. Stewed beef heart has a very pronounced flavor not liked by everyone.

Kidney The fat surrounding the kidneys produces the best suet for use in pastry. The fatty core, which is unappetizing, should be removed when the kidney is chopped for cooking. As the flavor is strong it is usually cooked together with some beef stew meat in proportions according to family preference for more or less kidney – usually two parts beef to one part kidney.

Liver Beef liver is the only liver not recommended to be panfried as it can be coarse and hard in texture. Like the kidney, it is better stewed with beef stew meat, and well flavored with onions. Soaking in milk for 2 hours before cooking does help to tenderize the liver and mellow the flavor. Some meat markets have what is known as baby-beef liver which comes from a young steer or heifer and is less strong than liver from a full-grown animal.

Oxtail One meaty oxtail should provide a meal for four when stewed for at least 3 hours. Undercooked oxtail is uneatable. A small oxtail makes a delicious meat soup.

Tongue Beef tongue has a surprisingly delicate flavor and texture. It weighs about 4 lb. and one average tongue can be curled around to fill a mold, but it is more necessary to cover and weight the mold than with the tongues from smaller animals which can be arranged exactly to fill the shape. You can buy beef tongues fresh, canned, pickled, or smoked.

Tripe This is in fact the muscular stomach lining of the animal; it is a creamy white very digestible meat but it requires lengthy cooking. Tripe is always partially cooked when you buy it but further simmering is necessary to tenderize it. The honeycomb is the preferred cut, other types are described as the blanket, monk's head, and book, coming from the part of the stomach which suggests the names from the shape.

VARIOUS USES FOR CUTS OF BEEF

The cuts most suitable for roasting are standing rump, rolled rump, standing rib roast, and rolled rib roast. Standing rump can be somewhat difficult to carve because the rump and the tail bone remain in the joint. If this cut is not from high-quality beef it is better braised. A better joint to buy for roasting is a rolled rump. It should be sewn with string, piercing the fat and lean so that the cut will remain compact during roasting. Standing rib is the prime joint for roasting and should contain at least two ribs and weigh about 4 lb. A rolled rib is a standing rib minus the bones and should not contain the parchment-like tissue between the ribs – all too often this is left in.

From the wholesale cut, sirloin, come various steaks each named for the shape of the bone it contains. Wedge-bone sirloin is the largest of the sirloin steaks, then the round-bone sirloin and double-bone sirloin; the latter contains proportionately more bone to lean meat as the steak contains a slice of the pelvis and a portion of the backbone. The pinbone sirloin somewhat resembles a porterhouse steak. Other steaks suitable for broiling or panfrying include T-bone steak, club steak, and rib steak. Since the cutting of sirloin steaks varies in different parts of the country it is difficult to say which cut of steak from the sirloin is the best to buy.

The cuts most suitable for cooking by the braising method include flank, plate, brisket, shank, chuck and blade pot-roast and top and bottom round steak.

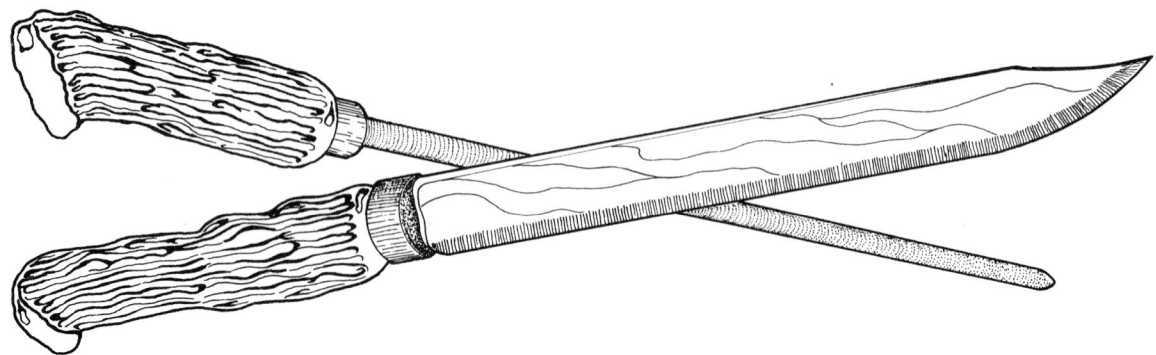

Cooking methods for cuts of beef

1 **Hind shank** Braising or soup-making.
2 **Top round** Braising.
3 **Rump** Rolled or standing rump – braising or roasting.
4 **Sirloin tip** Sometimes called knuckle roast – roasting or braising.
5 **Sirloin** Gives sirloin steaks for broiling or panbroiling.
6 **Loin** Gives T-bone, porterhouse steaks, fillet, and club steaks for broiling, panbroiling, and panfrying.
7 **Loin rib end and standing rib** Roasting, can be boned and rolled. Rib steaks – broiling, panbroiling, or panfrying.

8 **Chuck** Gives blade pot-roast, triangular pot-roast, boneless chuck roast and shoulder all suitable for braising. Can be cubed for casseroles etc.
9 **Boneless shoulder** Braising.
10 **Brisket** Gives corned beef and brisket for braising.
11 **Shank** or shank knuckle and cross-cut fore shanks. Braising and soup-making.
12 **Plate** Sometimes boned and rolled. Braising.
13 **Flank** (not shown) Can be stuffed, rolled, and braised. Sometimes scored – braising.

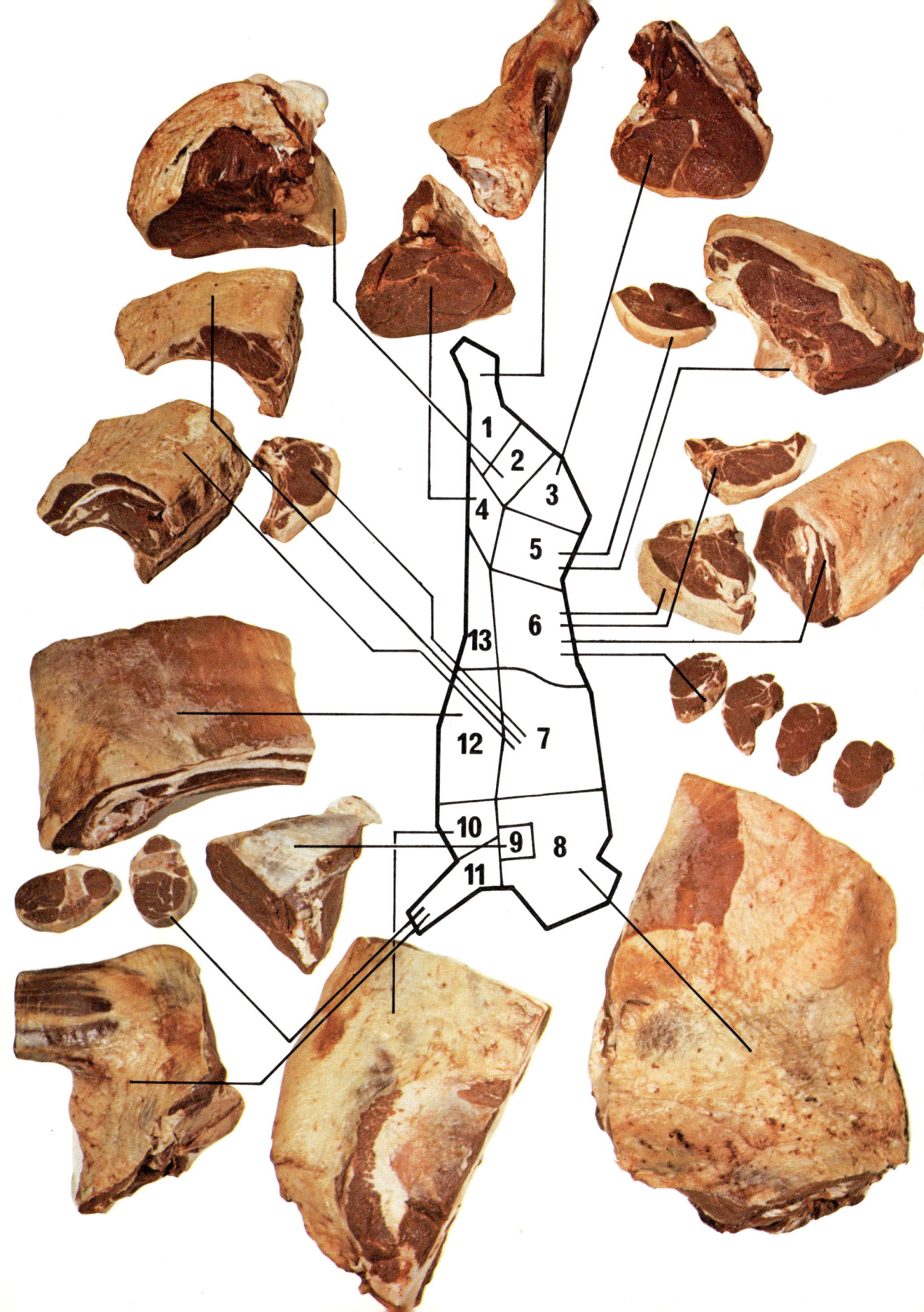

How to carve cooked beef joints

Standing rib roast Start at the outer edge of the fat and cut into the rib, making the slice as even as you can. The thickness of each slice depends on your family's preference. Hold the roast steady by inserting the fork in the side between the two top ribs. Remove each slice by cutting down right next to the rib.

Blade pot-roast When carving this cut remember to cut the slices across the grain of the meat. As this cut is always braised it is easy to separate the individual muscles. With a boning knife cut off one corner close to the bone as shown and remove this part. Place on its side, hold firmly with a fork and slice downwards across the grain. Treat the other muscles in the same way.

Rolled rib roast Place the roast on a platter or board with the cut surface downwards. Hold the roast steady with the fork and remove loop of string. If the roast has been tied correctly the string should be continuous throughout most of the cut and will pierce the fat in a line down one side. The string should be cut here and there and any little pieces remaining carefully removed. With a steady sawing action cut slices, across the grain of the meat, to the preferred thickness.

Other rolled roasts These are placed lengthwise on the platter. Hold the roast firmly with the fork and carve slices, across the grain, to the preferred thickness.

Carving steaks
Like most meat, steaks should be cut across the grain. If the steak contains a bone as in the case of a T-bone or porterhouse steak this should be removed as follows:
Place the steak on a platter or board with the tail of the steak to the left and with a small sharp carving knife or boning knife cut around the T-bone so finely that there is no meat adhering to it when it is removed. The steak can now be cut across making wedge-shaped portions. The tail is cut, as shown, into diagonal slices. This method makes serving very easy as each person can have a piece of tenderloin, a piece of the larger section and a piece of the tail and no one person is favored with a particular juicy piece.

Lamb

A lamb is a young sheep of either sex that has not reached maturity. Lambs for the meat market are divided into four groups:
Hothouse lamb raised carefully and slaughtered between six to ten weeks old. The supply of hothouse lambs is small and the meat from them is quite expensive.
Genuine spring lamb milk-fed lamb marketed in the spring and early summer.
Spring lamb lamb under fourteen months old marketed in the fall and winter. These lambs have subsisted on feed other than milk.
Yearling lamb a nearly mature animal between fifteen and twenty months old.

HOW TO CHOOSE LAMB

Generally speaking young lamb is pink with pale creamy or even white fat. As the animals get older, the flesh becomes redder and the fat darker in color. Very young animals sometimes have little flesh and it is better to choose small, plump joints for roasting to get a fair proportion of meat to bone. The exterior fat is covered with a parchment-like tissue called the fell. By the time the lamb reaches the meat counter the fell has usually been removed from all cuts but the leg. The fell makes no difference to the flavor of the meat, but marinade and other seasonings will penetrate more easily if the fell has been removed.

Lamb bones are porous and red. At the break joints (the point at which the feet are removed) in young lambs there are four red, moist, and porous ridges. In older lambs these ridges become hard and white.

VARIETY MEATS

Brains These are sold by the set, and as each set provides less than one good portion, they are often combined with eggs, or in ragoûts and soufflés with sweetbreads.
Heart A lamb heart, stuffed and roasted or braised makes a nice portion for one. It takes $2\frac{1}{2}$–3 hours to simmer or braise a lamb heart.
Kidney Lamb kidneys are each surrounded in fat which should be broken away, not cut off with a knife, or the kidney may be damaged. Remove the skin and center core before cooking. For panfrying or broiling cut in half. For a mixed grill the kidneys can be almost split through, opened out like a book and threaded with a wooden toothpick to hold open while cooking to give a butterfly effect. When done remove the toothpick and fill the kidney's center with a ball of softened butter mixed with chopped parsley, a squeeze of lemon juice, salt and pepper and a pinch of dry mustard. Allow two lamb kidneys per portion.
Liver Although much cheaper than calf liver, lamb liver is tender enough to treat in the same way, for panfrying and broiling. It becomes hard if overcooked and should be still slightly pink in the center. The main object in cooking it is to brown the exterior attractively and slightly solidify the center.
Sweetbreads Lamb sweetbreads are the most delicate and tender of all. Each pair serves one portion. Before cooking they should be soaked in cold water for 30–45 minutes and the water changed three times.
Tongue Lamb tongues are cooked in the same way as beef tongue but are never so tender when served hot. They are usually cooked salted to add more flavor, skinned and packed four or six at a time into one mold. The mold must be filled with a strong-setting stock or the shape of the mold will break up when it is turned out and sliced.

VARIOUS USES FOR CUTS OF LAMB

Lamb produces some very interesting show pieces for a dinner party. The rack of lamb can be used to make either a guard of honor (see page 64) or a crown roast (see page 64). The trimmings need not be wasted but should be simmered while the joint is roasting to provide stock for the gravy. As the butcher makes a considerable charge to prepare either of these for roasting, it is worth learning how to do it yourself. The rack can also be divided into rib chops which can if liked be made to look like saratoga chops – the rib and backbone are removed and the tail is rolled around the rib 'eye'. A skewer holds them in place. Rib chops can be Frenched in which case the bone must be protected, during cooking, with a piece of aluminum foil. Boneless leg steaks are ideal for kebabs.

Loin chops, English chops, blade chops, and arm chops are all suitable for broiling or panfrying; boneless shoulder chops are suitable for braising. The cuts to choose for roasting are the leg, rolled shoulder or breast, loin, or boneless sirloin roast. The leg can be Frenched by removing the meat on the shank, in which case aluminum foil must be used to protect the exposed bone. The square-cut shoulder can be roasted, but as you might imagine it is quite a difficult joint to carve. The cushion shoulder is an easier joint for carving as all the bones have been removed and the shoulder sewn together on the two open sides. You can ask the butcher to leave one side open so that you can add a stuffing. It will take 2–3 cups of stuffing depending on the size of the shoulder. Sew or skewer the opening after the shoulder has been stuffed. Ground lamb usually comes from the flank, breast, shank, and neck. It can be made into patties or combined with other ground meat for a meat loaf.

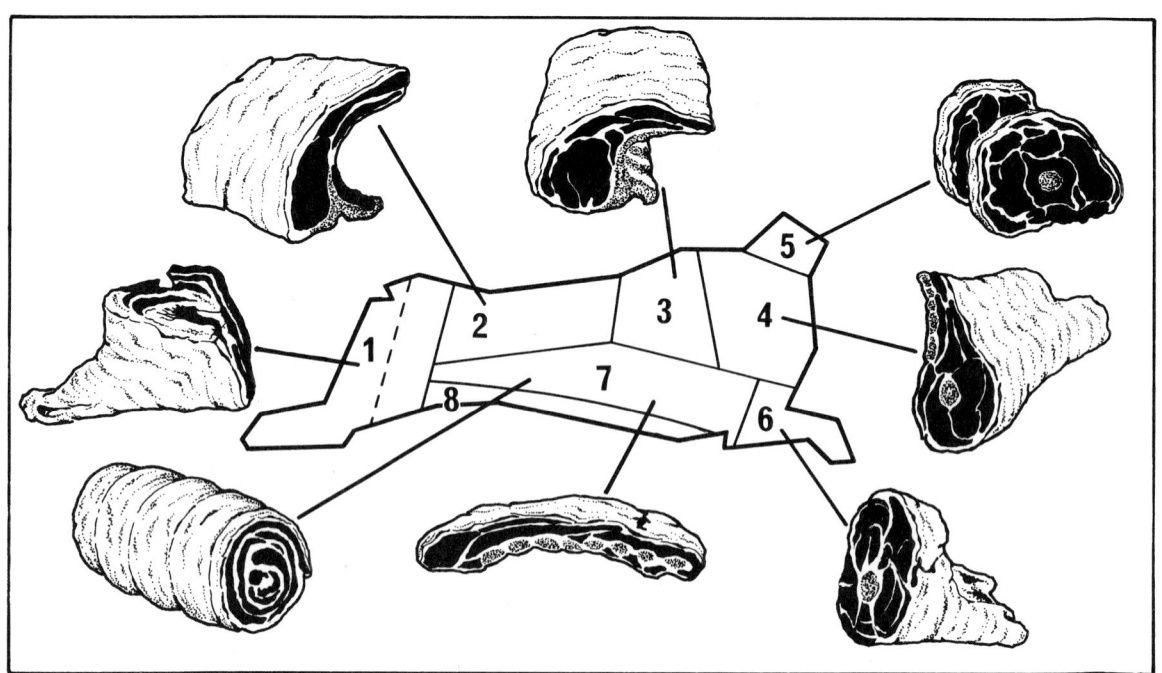

Cooking methods for cuts of lamb

1 **Leg** Gives American leg, Frenched leg, and boneless sirloin roast all suitable for roasting. Can be roasted whole or slices cut from the top for panbroiling or panfrying.
2 **Loin** Gives loin chops and English chops for broiling, panbroiling, and panfrying; loin roast can also be boned and rolled for roasting.
3 **Rack** Gives rib chops for broiling, panbroiling, and panfrying; rib roast can be formed into a crown roast.
4 **Shoulder** Gives square-cut shoulder and cushion shoulder for roasting, can be boned and rolled for roasting or braising. Boneless shoulder chops and saratoga chops for broiling, panbroiling, panfrying, or braising.
5 **Neck slices** Braising.
6 **Shank** Braising.
7 **Breast** Gives riblets for braising. Can be boned, stuffed, and rolled for roasting or braising.
8 **Flank** (not shown) Often discarded, or it may be ground or used for lamb stew meat.

New Zealand guard of honor (see page 64)

How to carve cooked lamb joints

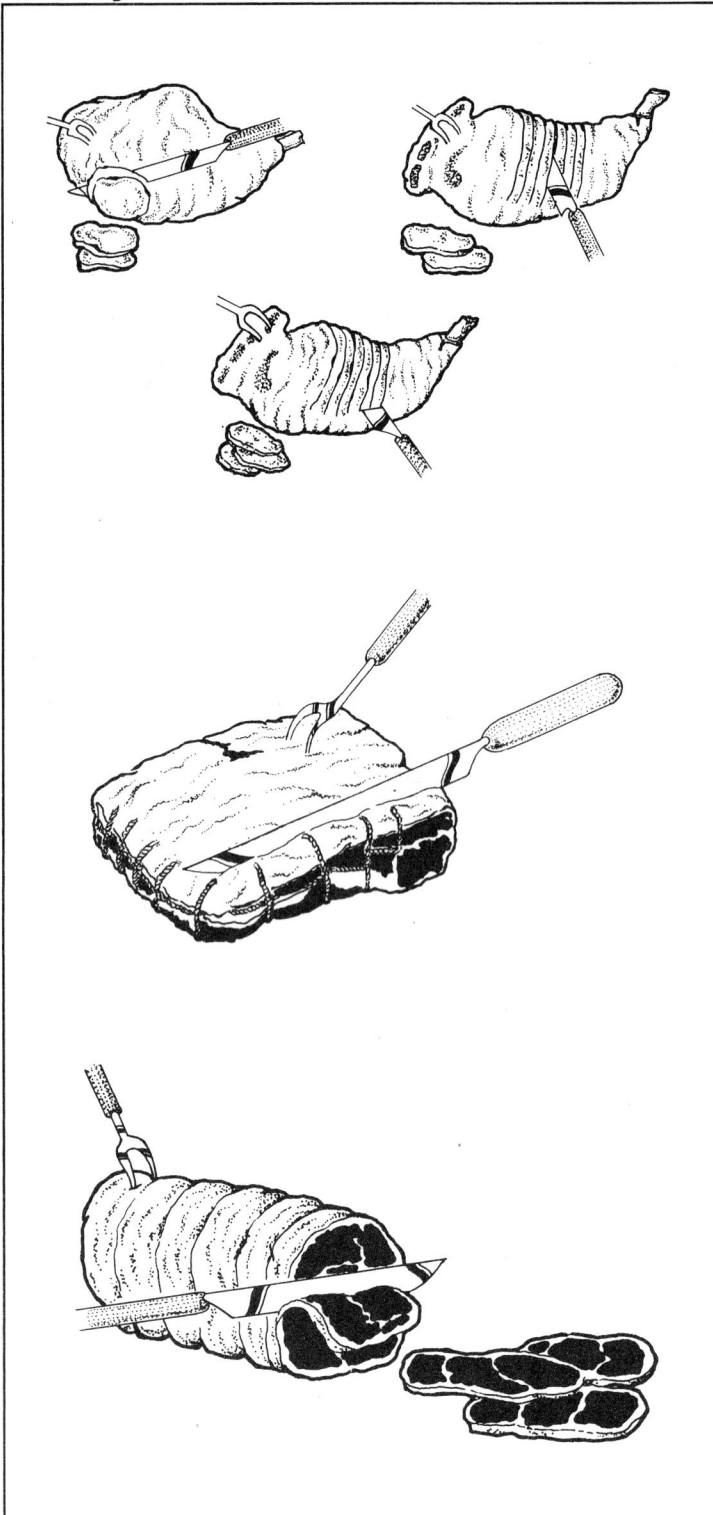

Leg of lamb Place on the platter with the leg bone to the right and remove two or three slices, lengthwise, from the thin side of the leg where the kneecap is. Turn the roast so that the flat side is on the platter. Make slices, perpendicular to the leg bone, starting where the shank joins the leg. Loosen the slices closely along the top of the bone so that they can be served easily.

Cushion shoulder Place on the platter. Hold the roast firmly with the fork and carve slices across the grain to the preferred thickness, removing the string or skewers as you carve.

Rolled roasts Place on the platter lengthwise. Hold the roast firmly with the fork and carve cross-grain slices to the preferred thickness.

For carving a **loin** see instructions under pork (page 32).

Pork

Pork is always a tender meat because, like lamb or veal, it comes from a young animal, and ranks next to beef in the amount consumed in the U.S.A. All pork joints provide very white delicate meat and can be roasted (and because of the pervasive fat the meat is virtually self-basting). Most of the pork you eat comes from animals between five to seven months of age which weigh 200–225 lb. when they come to market. Since the hogs are under a year old when slaughtered it makes no difference whether the meat comes from barrows (males castrated when young) or gilts (young females).

Pork does tend to deteriorate more quickly than other meats in a hot atmosphere so do take extra care that it is kept cool and covered at all times after you get it home. Do also be sure to cook pork thoroughly as there is a danger of a food poisoning peculiar to this one animal in under done meat.

HOW TO CHOOSE PORK

The meat from very young animals will have a delicate rose-pink flesh and very white fat. The only difference in meat from older animals is that the lean will be a deeper pink color (the darker the color the older the animal, though some breeds naturally yield a dark lean).

The fat should look firm but dry. If it is flabby or oily looking this again is a bad sign. The skin is thin and light colored in a young animal and becomes progressively thicker and darker in older pigs. The bones should be white with a pinkish tinge rather than yellowish. A small marbling of fat in the lean indicates a well-fed animal with tender flesh. Although good pork has a high proportion of fat this should never be wasted. It is very little trouble to render down slowly in a strong skillet. The strained fat, when set, is wonderful for pastry-making as well as for frying. To ensure that the skin makes good crackling, it must be scored either in parallel lines or in a diamond pattern so that the cooked skin breaks up into convenient pieces for carving and eating. If the skin has been removed because the layer of fat is too deep to make an attractive joint, you will get no crackling. If the surface of fat is sprinkled with salt and exposed to high heat for the first 10 minutes of roasting, the surface will be fairly crisp.

VARIETY MEATS

Pork variety meats are exceptionally strong-flavored and tasty without being expensive. They are useful for making pâtés and meat loaves.

Head Makes excellent brawn and the tongue can be salted, boned, and boiled.

Kidney Very strongly flavored but quite tender; young pork kidneys can be broiled and larger ones are suitable for use in terrines, braises, and stews. Two small kidneys are sufficient for one portion.

Liver Some people dislike the strong flavor of pork liver, but if soaked in milk or a marinade for 2 hours before broiling or panfrying it becomes tender.

Trotters In old country recipes, the trotters are usually cooked with other meat from the pig to give a good setting quality to brawn. The meat is gelatinous but very tender and if boiled until soft enough to bone, the trotters can be stuffed and broiled or panfried. Allow one trotter per portion.

VARIOUS USES FOR CUTS OF PORK

The hind leg is usually large enough to be cut into two or even three good roasting joints. Slices from the top end can be broiled and panfried, as for pork chops. The loin, which gives the prime joint for roasting, may be cut into chops, with the skin and surplus fat removed. The most economical roasting joint, the foreleg – also called picnic – can be boned, rolled, and stuffed. The flank always tends to be a fat joint. All cuts are sufficiently tender to make good kebabs as long as they are not too fat. Spareribs are the rib bones which still have a certain amount of meat and are usually cooked in a barbecue sauce. Some of the meat from the pig is utilized in making pork sausages; most sausages are a mixture of pork and beef, or pork, beef, and veal, plus seasonings. Sausages are divided into two large groups – fresh and dry. Good quality sausages make an appetizing and reasonably-priced family meal.

The most often cured meat in the U.S.A. is pork and the packing houses guard their secrets of curing and smoking carefully. The cured and smoked meats from the packing houses include ham (butt half) and ham (shank half) and smoked picnic shoulder.

How to salt or pickle pork

Fat back or other thin pieces of fat pork can be salted and pickled.

Cut the fat back into pieces about 6 inches square and rub each piece, on all sides, well with pickling salt. Pack the salted pork tightly in a clean crock (made of stoneware, pottery or glass) and leave it to stand in a cool place for 12 hours. For each 25 lb. meat make up the following brine and allow it to cool: $2\frac{1}{2}$ lb. salt, $\frac{1}{2}$ oz. saltpeter and 4 quarts boiling water. Pour the cooled brine over the meat so that it is completely covered with the brine. Store the pork, weighted and covered, in a cool place until ready to use.

How to dry-cure ham

Spread pieces of ham out on racks, making sure that they do not overlap. Sprinkle very lightly with salt – do not cover them heavily with salt at this stage. For every 10 lb. ham allow the following salt mixture: 1 cup salt, $\frac{1}{4}$ cup sugar, 2 teaspoons sodium nitrate with 2 bay leaves, 2 coriander seeds, 3 cloves and 6 peppercorns crushed in a mortar. Rub the ham repeatedly with the salt mixture, ensuring that the entire surface is covered well. Then pack in the salt mixture.

The salt and pepper act as preservatives, the sugar adds flavor and the sodium nitrate helps to give the meat a good color. To ensure effective salt-penetration allow 3 days for each pound of meat per piece. Boned hams and smaller pieces will of course cure more quickly. Salt-penetration is slowed to a standstill in freezing temperatures therefore if the temperature drops be sure to add an equal length of time to the curing period.

Cooking methods for cuts of pork

1 **Fresh ham** Gives ham, butt and shank half, fresh ham roast and rolled fresh ham roast, all suitable for roasting; ham butt slice and center ham slice for broiling, pan-broiling or panfrying.
2 **Loin** Gives sirloin roast, boneless sirloin roast, loin roast, and loin blade roast; rib and loin chops for panfrying or braising. The tenderloin can be roasted whole or slices can be panfried.
3 **Boston butt** Gives blade steaks for braising or panfrying. Boston butt suitable for roasting – can also be boned and rolled.
4 **Trotter** Only suitable for long, slow simmering.
5 **Jowl** Gives the jowl bacon square – can be cooked whole or in slices, panfried, braised, or boiled.
6 **Picnic** Gives cushion picnic shoulder and fresh picnic shoulder for roasting. Picnic shoulder can be boned and rolled. Shoulder hocks for braising and cooking in liquid; arm steaks for braising and panfrying.
7, 8 **Belly** Gives spareribs and side. Spareribs for roasting, barbecuing, or simmering. The side is cured to make bacon for broiling and panfrying.
9 **Fat back** (not shown) May be salted to give salt pork or rendered down to produce lard.

Cuts of pork

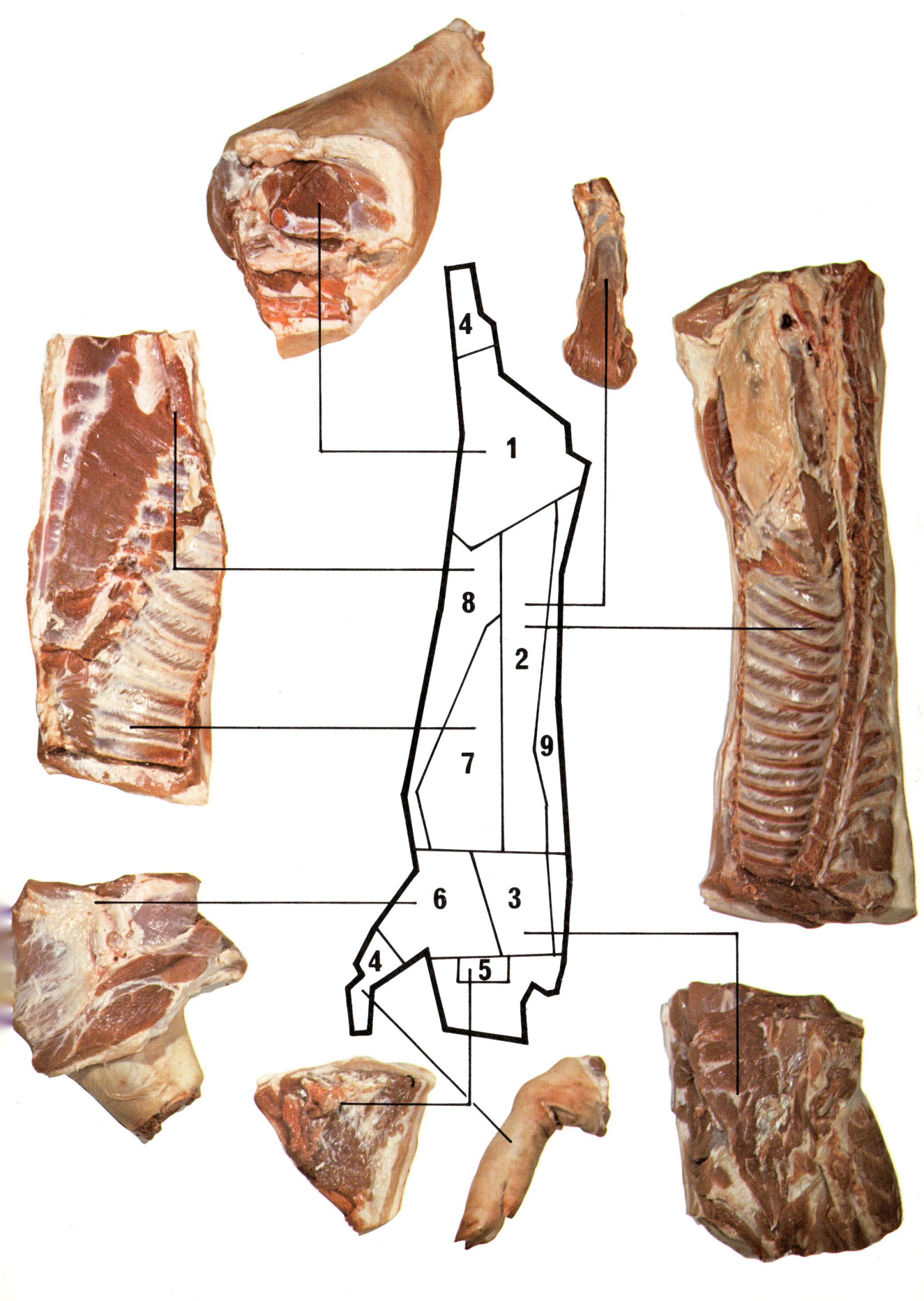

How to carve cooked pork joints

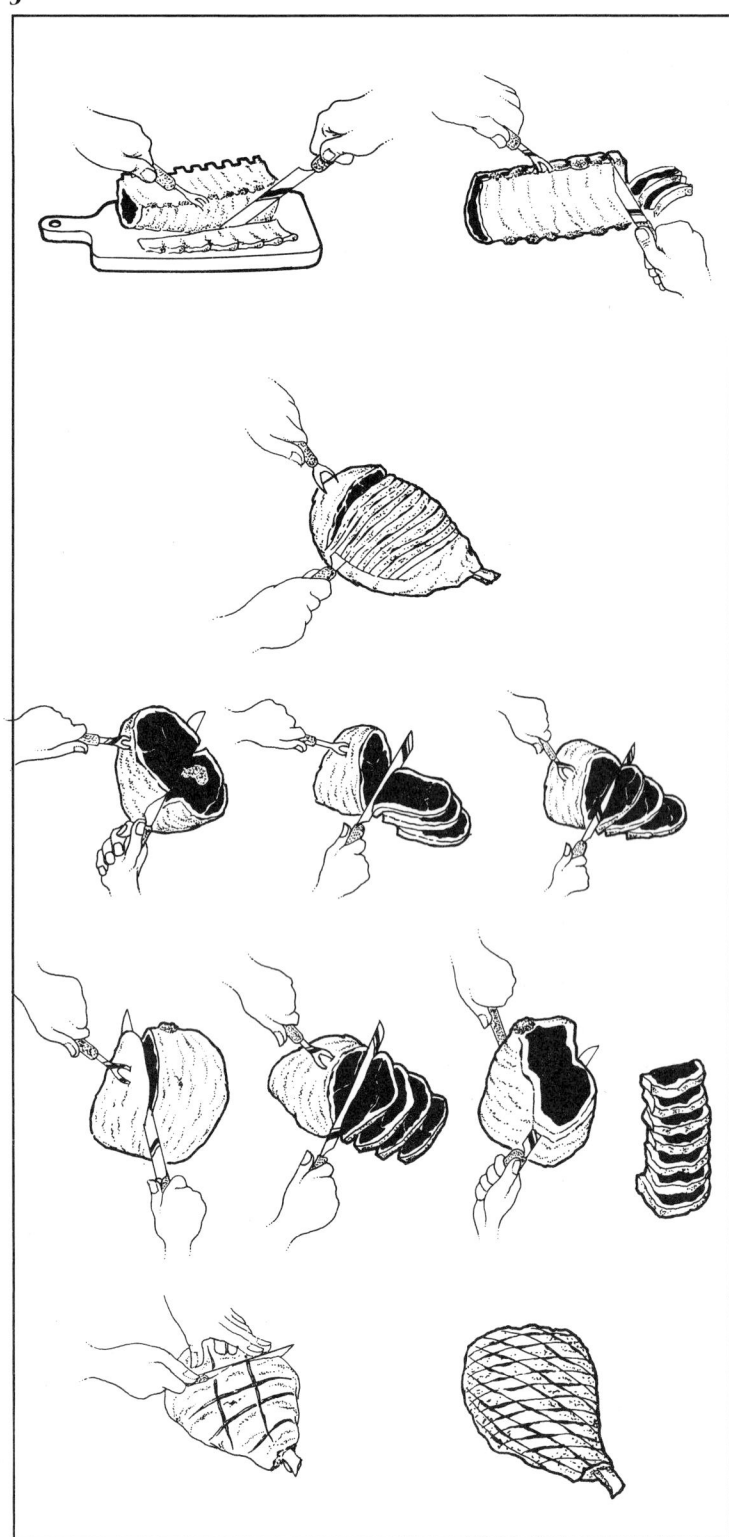

Loin roast Remove the backbone before bringing the roast to the table so that no meat is lost with the bone. Place the roast on the platter with the rib side facing you so that you can see the angle and slice accurately. Hold the fork on top of the roast to keep it steady. Cut closely along each side of the rib bone. One slice will contain the rib and the next one will be boneless.

Whole ham Remove two or three slices lengthwise from the thin side of the leg where the kneecap is. Turn the joint so that the flattened side sits on the platter. Hold the ham steady with the fork and make slices, starting where the shank joins the leg, making perpendicular slices to the leg bone. Loosen slices closely along the top of the leg bone so that they can be easily removed for serving.

Ham shank half Place the joint on the platter with the shank to your left and turn the ham so that the thick 'cushion' side is upwards. Cut along the top of the leg and shank bones. Using a sharp boning knife, cut around the leg and remove all the meat. Turn the meat to the thickest side and cut in slices.

Ham butt half Place the ham butt half on the platter, face down. Hold the joint steady with the fork and cut down along the bone to remove the large boneless section. Place the boneless section on another platter and carve in cross-grain slices. Hold the remaining section of the butt securely, with the meaty side to your right. Cut in slices across the meat until the knife strikes the bone. Release each slice from the bone with the tip of the knife and remove to the side of the platter.

Scoring ham
The rind on the cut need not necessarily be peeled off. Score it, before cooking, with a sharp-pointed knife in a diamond pattern, and rub coarse salt well into the scoring; this produces a flavorful and crisp rind.

Cooking for the family

If economy is the chief consideration in catering for family meals, this does not mean that they need be repetitive and boring. By making more use of cheaper cuts and a variety of cooking methods, a different menu can be presented every day for weeks on end.

Veal and marrow casserole

IMPERIAL	AMERICAN
1 lb. pie veal	1 lb. boneless veal
2 tablespoons corn oil	3 tablespoons corn oil
1 medium-sized marrow	1 medium-sized summer squash
1 onion	1 onion
1 teaspoon dried mixed herbs	1 teaspoon dried mixed herbs
1 15-oz. can mushroom soup	1 15-oz. can mushroom soup
salt and pepper to taste	salt and pepper to taste

Cut the veal into 1-inch cubes and sauté in the hot oil in a flameproof casserole until lightly browned. Remove from the heat and add the peeled, de-seeded and diced marrow, the peeled and sliced onion, the herbs, soup and seasoning, mixing thoroughly. Cook in a moderate oven, 350°F, 180°C, Gas Mark 4, for 1–1½ hours until the veal is tender. Serve with rice.

Veal and corn pie*

IMPERIAL	AMERICAN
1 lb. boned veal shoulder or leg	1 lb. boneless veal shoulder
1 oz. seasoned flour	¼ cup seasoned flour
2 tablespoons corn oil	3 tablespoons corn oil
1 medium-sized onion	1 medium-sized onion
2 tablespoons tomato purée	3 tablespoons tomato paste
¾ pint stock	scant 2 cups stock
1 10-oz. can sweetcorn	1 10-oz. can kernel corn
8 oz. short crust pastry	basic pie dough using 2 cups all-purpose flour etc.

Cut the veal into small pieces and toss in seasoned flour. Sauté in the hot oil until lightly browned. Peel and slice the onion and cook with the meat until slightly softened. Stir in the tomato purée and stock and place in a suitable pie dish. Cover with foil and cook in a moderately hot oven, 375°F, 190°C, Gas Mark 5, for 1¼–1½ hours, until the veal is tender. Add the drained sweetcorn and cool. Roll out the pastry to fit the dish and place over the filling. Trim the edges and make a small hole in the centre for the steam to escape. Return to a hot oven, 425°F, 220°C, Gas Mark 7, for 15–20 minutes or until golden brown.

* Freeze baked or unbaked, wrapped in foil. Do not cut steam vent if freezing unbaked. Defrost and bake as above, or reheat in a hot oven for 30 minutes.

Spring veal casserole

IMPERIAL	AMERICAN
1 lb. best end of neck veal chops	1 lb. veal chops
3 rashers streaky bacon	3 bacon slices
1 tablespoon oil	1 tablespoon oil
1 oz. butter	2 tablespoons butter
1 medium-sized onion, chopped	1 medium-sized onion, chopped
1 clove garlic, crushed	1 clove garlic, crushed
8 oz. carrots, chopped	½ lb. carrots, chopped
8 oz. leeks, sliced	½ lb. leeks, sliced
8 oz. tomatoes, skinned and chopped	½ lb. tomatoes, skinned and chopped
few sprigs rosemary	few sprigs rosemary
salt and pepper to taste	salt and pepper to taste

Ask the butcher for the trimmings when he chines and cuts the chops for you, boil these to make stock for the casserole. De-rind the bacon and cut into small pieces. Heat the oil and butter in a frying pan and sauté the bacon, onion and garlic until beginning to brown, then transfer to a casserole. Sauté carrots and leeks in the remaining oil and add to the casserole with the tomatoes. Brown the chops on both sides in the frying pan, place on top of the vegetables, pour over the stock and sprinkle with rosemary, salt and pepper. Cover and cook in a moderate oven, 350°F, 180°C, Gas Mark 4, for 1 hour or until the meat and vegetables are tender. Serve with buttered new potatoes or noodles.

Potted hough

IMPERIAL	AMERICAN
1 knuckle of veal	about 3 lb. shin bone of veal
8 oz. shin of beef, in pieces	½ lb. boneless shank knuckle, in pieces
1 teaspoon salt	1 teaspoon salt
2 bay leaves	2 bay leaves
6 peppercorns	6 peppercorns
6 allspice	6 allspice

Ask your butcher to saw through the veal bone in several places and place in a saucepan with the beef. Cover with water, add the salt and spices and bring to the boil. Simmer very gently for 2–3 hours. Drain the meat and boil the stock uncovered until reduced to approximately ½ pint (U.S. 1¼ cups). Remove the meat from the bones, shred roughly and pack into a loaf tin or mould. Strain the reduced liquid and pour over the meat. Leave in a cool place to set. Turn out and serve sliced, with salad.

Steak and kidney pudding*

IMPERIAL	AMERICAN
Suet pastry:	*Suet crust:*
4 oz. shredded suet	¼ lb. beef suet, finely chopped
8 oz. self-raising flour	2 cups all-purpose flour sifted with 2¼ teaspoons baking powder
pinch salt	pinch salt
pinch pepper	pinch pepper
water to mix	water to mix
Filling:	*Filling:*
12 oz.–1 lb. stewing steak, cubed	¾–1 lb. beef stew meat, cubed
2–3 lamb's kidneys or 4 oz. ox kidney, cut into pieces	2–3 lamb kidneys or ¼ lb. beef kidney, cut into pieces
2 tablespoons seasoned flour	3 tablespoons seasoned flour
beef stock or water, or half stock and red wine	beef stock or water or half stock and red wine

Mix together suet, flour and seasoning with sufficient water to make a firm dough. Roll out two-thirds of the pastry and use to line a 2-pint pudding basin. Arrange meat and kidney in layers, sprinkling each layer with seasoned flour. Pour over sufficient stock to come three-quarters of the way up the basin. Roll out remaining pastry to form a lid, moisten edges and seal well together. Cover securely with foil or greaseproof paper and steam or boil for 4 hours.

* To freeze, when completely cold, cover with freezer foil and label. To defrost and reheat, boil or steam for 1 hour.

Cut off two-thirds of the suet pastry and use to line a 2-pint pudding basin. Cube the stewing steak and cut the kidney into pieces.

Place the prepared meat and kidney in layers in the lined basin. Sprinkle each layer with seasoned flour. Add stock to come three-quarters of the way up the basin.

Serve the steak and kidney pudding from the basin. The sides of the basin can be covered with a white napkin folded diagonally and wrapped round it.

Pork and leek pudding*

IMPERIAL	AMERICAN
suet pastry, see opposite	suet crust, see opposite
Filling:	*Filling:*
12 oz. lean blade bone of pork, diced	¾ lb. pork stew meat, diced
3 leeks, sliced	3 leeks, sliced
2 tablespoons seasoned flour	3 tablespoons seasoned flour
1 teaspoon dried sage	1 teaspoon dried sage
chicken stock or water	chicken stock or water

Line a 2-pint pudding basin with suet pastry as opposite. Arrange meat and leeks in layers, sprinkling each layer with seasoned flour and sage. Pour over sufficient stock to come three-quarters of the way up the pudding. Cover and steam or boil as for steak and kidney pudding.

* To freeze follow instructions for previous recipe.

Pork loaf*

IMPERIAL	AMERICAN
8 oz. blade bone of pork, cooked	½ lb. pork stew meat, cooked
4 oz. streaky bacon	¼ lb. bacon slices
2 oz. cooked long-grain rice	scant ½ cup cooked long-grain rice
salt and pepper to taste	salt and pepper to taste
1 egg	1 egg
½ packet sage and onion stuffing	½ package sage and onion stuffing

Mince the pork and bacon. Mix together with the rice, seasoning and beaten egg. Make up the stuffing according to the packet instructions, stir into the meat and mix thoroughly. Grease a loaf tin and press in the mixture firmly, cover with greased foil and bake in a moderately hot oven, 375°F, 190°C, Gas Mark 5, for 35–40 minutes. Serve hot or cold with vegetables.

* To freeze follow instructions opposite.

Devonshire meat loaf*

IMPERIAL	AMERICAN
1 oz. butter	2 tablespoons butter
1 medium-sized onion, chopped	1 medium-sized onion, chopped
1 carrot, sliced	1 carrot, sliced
4 oz. mushrooms, chopped	¼ lb. mushrooms, sliced
1 lb. minced beef	1 lb. ground beef
8 oz. fresh white breadcrumbs	4 cups fresh soft bread crumbs
4 oz. shredded suet	scant 1 cup finely chopped beef suet
2 tablespoons chopped parsley	3 tablespoons chopped parsley
pinch mixed dried herbs	pinch mixed dried herbs
salt and pepper to taste	salt and pepper to taste
1 egg, lightly beaten	1 egg, lightly beaten
3 rashers streaky bacon	3 bacon slices

Melt the butter and fry onion, carrot and mushrooms until soft. Add minced beef and fry, stirring constantly, until browned. Remove mixture from heat and combine with breadcrumbs, suet, herbs and seasoning and bind with the beaten egg. De-rind bacon and stretch with the back of a knife. Use to line the base of a lightly greased 2-lb. loaf tin. Place mixture in tin, press down well and bake in a moderately hot oven, 400°F, 200°C, Gas Mark 6, for 30 minutes. Serve hot or cold.

* To freeze before baking, cool in tin, cover with foil and label. Defrost in the refrigerator overnight and bake as above. To freeze baked, cool, cover and label. Defrost, covered, and reheat in a moderate oven, 350°F, 180°C, Gas Mark 4, for 25 minutes.

Holiday barbecued lamb

IMPERIAL	AMERICAN
1 clove garlic	1 clove garlic
1 leg of lamb, about 3–4 lb.	1 lamb leg, about 3–4 lb.
1 teaspoon lemon juice	1 teaspoon lemon juice
grated nutmeg to taste	grated nutmeg to taste
Sauce:	*Sauce:*
1 oz. butter	2 tablespoons butter
1 small onion, chopped	1 small onion, chopped
4 oz. mushrooms, finely chopped	¼ lb. mushrooms, finely chopped
½ pint canned tomato juice	1¼ cups canned tomato juice
1 tablespoon Worcestershire sauce	1 tablespoon Worcestershire sauce
1 tablespoon vinegar	1 tablespoon vinegar
bouquet garni	bouquet garni
1 tablespoon lemon juice	1 tablespoon lemon juice
¼ pint apple purée	⅔ cup applesauce

Cut the garlic in half and rub the cut surface over the skin of the lamb, then reserve. Sprinkle over the lemon juice and grated nutmeg. Weigh the lamb, place in a roasting pan and cook according to the chart on page 9. To make the sauce, melt the butter in a small saucepan and fry the onion gently and remaining garlic until the onion is soft but not coloured. Stir in the mushrooms, tomato juice, Worcestershire sauce and vinegar. Add the bouquet garni and adjust seasoning. Bring to the boil and simmer for about 3 minutes. Add the lemon juice and apple purée, return to the boil and simmer gently for 20 minutes. Remove the bouquet garni before serving with the roast lamb.

35

Beef chain with an economy cut

Basic mince

IMPERIAL	AMERICAN
3 tablespoons corn oil	scant ¼ cup corn oil
2 large onions, finely chopped	2 large onions, finely chopped
2 large carrots, sliced	2 large carrots, sliced
5 lb. minced beef	5 lb. ground beef
1 beef stock cube	1 beef bouillon cube
2 teaspoons salt	2 teaspoons salt
½ teaspoon pepper	½ teaspoon pepper
1 teaspoon dried mixed herbs	1 teaspoon dried mixed herbs

Heat the oil in a large saucepan, fry the onion and carrot in it gently until soft but not coloured. Add the meat and fry, stirring, until it changes colour. Add the crumbled stock cube, seasoning and herbs and sufficient water just to cover. Bring to the boil, cover and simmer for 45 minutes. Divide the cooked mince into three equal portions.

1 Beef Marguerite

IMPERIAL	AMERICAN
1 tablespoon seedless raisins	1 tablespoon seedless raisins
1 portion basic mince	1 portion basic mince
2 hard-boiled eggs	2 hard-cooked eggs
12 large croûtons, see page 76	12 large croûtons, see page 76
1 tablespoon chopped parsley	1 tablespoon chopped parsley

Stir raisins into basic mince while still hot. Pour this mixture into a warm serving dish. Arrange wedges of hard-boiled eggs like the petals of a daisy round the top.

Place the croûtons in the centre and sprinkle with parsley before serving with vegetables or a green salad.

2 Mince and mushroom crumble

IMPERIAL	AMERICAN
1 portion basic mince	1 portion basic mince
1 oz. butter or margarine	2 tablespoons butter or margarine
4 oz. mushrooms, sliced	¼ lb. mushrooms, sliced
Topping:	Topping:
salt and pepper to taste	salt and pepper to taste
2 teaspoons mixed dried herbs	2 teaspoons mixed dried herbs
6 oz. plain flour	1½ cups all-purpose flour
3 oz. butter or margarine	scant ½ cup butter or margarine
1 oz. fresh white breadcrumbs	½ cup fresh soft bread crumbs

Defrost the mince if necessary. Melt the fat in a saucepan and gently fry the mushrooms until softened. Stir in the mince sufficiently to blend, but not to reheat. Spoon into a pie dish. Make the topping by mixing together the salt, pepper and herbs and stirring into the flour. Rub in the fat until the mixture resembles crumbs and then stir in the fresh breadcrumbs. Spoon this mixture over the mince, press down lightly and bake in the centre of a moderately hot oven, 375°F, 190°C, Gas Mark 5, for 45 minutes.

3 Duchess mince

IMPERIAL	AMERICAN
1 pie dish basic mince	1 pie dish basic mince
½ oz. butter	1 tablespoon butter
little warm milk	little warm milk
8 oz. cooked mashed potato	1 cup cooked mashed potato
salt and pepper to taste	salt and pepper to taste
good pinch grated nutmeg	good pinch grated nutmeg

Remove the foil covering from the mince and reheat in a hot oven, 425°F, 220°C, Gas Mark 7, for 30 minutes. Beat butter and sufficient warm milk into sieved cooked potato to make a good piping consistency. Season with salt, pepper and nutmeg to taste. Using a rose nozzle, pipe rosettes of potato to cover the surface of the mince. Return to the oven for about 10 minutes to brown the potatoes.

Cook the mince in bulk and freeze in a number of foil containers. To reheat after freezing remove the foil covering from the mince mixture.

Beat the butter and warm milk into the sieved cooked potato and pipe the mashed potato in rosettes over the surface of the mince.

Place in a hot oven for about 10 minutes to brown the potatoes. Serve the duchess mince from the foil containers, with vegetables.

Beef and chestnut ragoût*

IMPERIAL	AMERICAN
1 lb. stewing steak	1 lb. beef stew meat
2 tablespoons seasoned flour	3 tablespoons seasoned flour
2 tablespoons corn oil	3 tablespoons corn oil
2 medium-sized onions, chopped	2 medium-sized onions, chopped
1 pint beef stock	2½ cups beef stock
1 small head celery	1 small bunch celery
4 oz. chestnuts, boiled and peeled	¼ lb. chestnuts, boiled and peeled
few juniper berries (optional)	few juniper berries (optional)

Cut the meat into neat cubes, trimming off any surplus fat, and toss in the seasoned flour. Sauté the meat in the oil until sealed on all sides. Add the onions to the pan, and sauté with the meat until soft. Stir in the remaining flour, add the stock and bring to the boil, stirring. Cover and simmer for about 1½ hours. Wash and chop the celery finely, add to the meat with the chestnuts and juniper berries. Simmer for a further 35–40 minutes or until tender.

* To freeze, pack in any suitable container; defrost and reheat to serve.

Family beefburgers

IMPERIAL	AMERICAN
1 lb. minced beef	1 lb. ground beef
1 tablespoon tomato purée	1 tablespoon tomato paste
good pinch garlic salt	good pinch garlic salt
pinch black pepper	pinch black pepper
pinch nutmeg	pinch nutmeg
pinch mace	pinch mace
1 tablespoon chopped parsley	1 tablespoon chopped parsley
1 oz. fresh white breadcrumbs	½ cup fresh soft bread crumbs
1 egg, lightly beaten	1 egg, lightly beaten
2 tablespoons oil	3 tablespoons oil

Combine the meat, tomato purée, herbs, spices and seasonings and mix together well. Add the breadcrumbs and finally bind with the egg. Divide the mixture into eight and form into round flat cakes with floured hands. Heat the oil in a heavy frying pan and brown the beefburgers on each side over high heat. Reduce the heat and cook gently for 7–10 minutes on each side. Serve with onion rings in soft bread rolls together with a green salad.

Chilli con carne

IMPERIAL	AMERICAN
2 medium-sized onions	2 medium-sized onions
2 tablespoons oil	3 tablespoons oil
$1\frac{1}{2}$ lb. minced beef	$1\frac{1}{2}$ lb. ground beef
2 tablespoons tomato purée	3 tablespoons tomato paste
$\frac{3}{4}$ pint water	scant 2 cups water
salt and pepper to taste	salt and pepper to taste
$\frac{1}{2}$–1 teaspoon chilli powder	$\frac{1}{2}$–1 teaspoon chili powder
1 16-oz. can red kidney beans	1 16-oz. can red kidney beans

Peel and chop the onions and fry in the hot oil until brown. Remove from pan and brown meat in the remaining oil, replace onions and add tomato purée, water, seasoning and chilli powder. Bring to the boil, cover and simmer for 1–$1\frac{1}{2}$ hours. Add the drained kidney beans and simmer for a further 10 minutes.

Beef in spiced cider*

IMPERIAL	AMERICAN
2 lb. leg beef, cut in 1-inch pieces	2 lb. beef stew meat, cut in 1-inch pieces
2 tablespoons seasoned cornflour	3 tablespoons seasoned cornstarch
3 cloves	3 cloves
2 bay leaves	2 bay leaves
3 peppercorns	3 peppercorns
good pinch powdered mace or nutmeg	good pinch powdered mace or nutmeg
$\frac{1}{2}$ pint dry cider	$1\frac{1}{4}$ cups cider
8 oz. small onions	$\frac{1}{2}$ lb. small onions
2 large carrots, thickly sliced	2 large carrots, thickly sliced
2 dessert apples, cored and quartered	2 dessert apples, cored and quartered
$\frac{1}{4}$ pint stock	$\frac{2}{3}$ cup stock

Turn meat in seasoned cornflour. Put the cloves, bay leaves, peppercorns and mace in a flameproof casserole with the cider. Bring slowly to the boil, take from heat and allow to cool. Remove spices with a slotted draining spoon and add the meat to the cider, together with the onions, carrots and apples. Pour over the stock, bring to the boil, cover, and simmer gently for 2 hours or until meat is tender. If a thicker stew is liked, moisten remaining cornflour with a little cold water, stir in gently and cook for a further 3 minutes. (*Serves 6.*)

* To save valuable storage space, pack the solid ingredients of the stew into a suitable-sized container and fill up with just sufficient gravy to cover, allowing the necessary headspace before sealing. This ensures that a meal for three or six can be stored in a relatively small container and a little extra stock, made with a stock cube, can always be added when reheating.

Pot-roast of brisket

IMPERIAL	AMERICAN
2 teaspoons dry mustard	2 teaspoons dry mustard
2 tablespoons vinegar	3 tablespoons vinegar
3 tablespoons tomato purée	scant $\frac{1}{4}$ cup tomato paste
2 tablespoons corn oil	3 tablespoons corn oil
1 small onion, chopped	1 small onion, chopped
2 teaspoons brown sugar	2 teaspoons brown sugar
1 teaspoon dried sweet herbs	1 teaspoon dried sweet herbs
salt and pepper to taste	salt and pepper to taste
$\frac{1}{2}$ oz. dripping	1 tablespoon drippings
$2\frac{1}{2}$–3 lb. joint silverside or brisket	$2\frac{1}{2}$–3 lb. piece fresh brisket
3 large onions, quartered	3 large onions, quartered
3 large carrots, quartered	3 large carrots, quartered
2 teaspoons cornflour	2 teaspoons cornstarch

Mix mustard with vinegar. Add next six ingredients and mix well together to make a sauce. Heat the dripping in a heavy saucepan and brown the joint all over. Add the onions and carrots round the joint and pour the sauce over the meat. Cover with a close-fitting lid and simmer for $2\frac{1}{2}$–3 hours until meat is tender. Remove joint to a warm serving dish, surround with the vegetables, thicken the juices in the pan with the cornflour moistened with a little cold water and pour over the meat. (*Serves 6.*)

Boiled beef and carrots

IMPERIAL	AMERICAN
3 lb. joint salted silverside	3 lb. piece uncooked corned beef
8 peppercorns	8 peppercorns
2 cloves	2 cloves
1 teaspoon mixed dried herbs	1 teaspoon mixed dried herbs
6 carrots	6 carrots
4 onions	4 onions
Dumplings:	*Dumplings:*
8 oz. plain flour	2 cups all-purpose flour
salt and pepper to taste	salt and pepper to taste
1 teaspoon baking powder	1 teaspoon baking powder
4 oz. suet	scant 1 cup finely chopped beef suet
Garnish:	*Garnish:*
parsley sprigs	parsley sprigs

Tie the meat into a neat shape, put into a large saucepan and cover with cold water. Bring to the boil, add peppercorns, cloves and herbs tied together in a piece of muslin, cover pan and simmer for $1\frac{3}{4}$ hours. Peel carrots and onions and add to the pan. Simmer for a further 10 minutes. Sieve flour, seasoning and baking powder together, add suet and mix well. Add enough cold water to make a soft dough. Shape into six balls, add to the pan and simmer for a further 30 minutes. Place meat on a large serving dish and arrange carrots, onions and dumplings around. Garnish with sprigs of parsley.

New methods of roasting

With the need to use medium rather than prime cuts for roasting, on grounds of economy, more care in cooking is required. To keep joints tender, try this method of roasting in a transparent bag proof against oven heat. It retains all the juices, and is self-basting. A ring or twist tie fastens the bag loosely round the joint, and the bag is slit with a knife along the top to withdraw the cooked meat. To judge whether meat is done to your taste, a meat thermometer is an invaluable gadget. Either put in place before cooking, or insert towards end of cooking time as it registers within a few minutes. It can be inserted through a roasting bag, piercing it near the top to prevent juices running out.

Beef sauerbraten

IMPERIAL	AMERICAN
3½–4 lb. joint silverside	3½–4 lb. piece fresh brisket
salt and pepper	salt and pepper
½ pint wine vinegar	1¼ cups wine vinegar
½ pint water	1¼ cups water
1 clove garlic	1 clove garlic
2 carrots, halved	2 carrots, halved
2 large onions, sliced	2 large onions, sliced
2 bay leaves	2 bay leaves
10 peppercorns	10 peppercorns
3 oz. demerara sugar	6 tablespoons brown sugar
3 cloves	3 cloves
flour	flour
2 oz. bacon fat or lard	¼ cup bacon drippings or lard
1 carton soured cream	1 carton sour cream
chopped parsley	chopped parsley

Season meat with the salt and pepper and place in a large bowl. Bring vinegar and water to the boil, add garlic, carrots, onions, bay leaves, peppercorns, sugar and cloves. Pour this marinade over the beef, cover and leave in a cool place overnight. Remove meat and pat dry with a clean cloth. Reserve marinade. Sprinkle meat with flour. In a heavy saucepan, heat the bacon fat or lard, add meat and brown all over. Add about half the marinade, cover and simmer until meat is tender, about 2½–3 hours. Remove meat to serving dish and keep hot. Thicken gravy if desired with 1 tablespoon flour and water blended. Stir in soured cream, reheat gently (do not boil) and serve poured over the meat. Garnish with the parsley. (*Serves 6 hot.*)

Insert the meat thermometer into the joint prior to roasting. Alternatively it can be inserted towards the end of cooking time – through the bag.

Place the joint in a roasting bag ready for roasting. This method of roasting retains all the meat juices and is self-basting.

When the joint is cooked slit the bag and remove the joint. Make the gravy in the normal way with the juices which have collected in the bag.

Add peppercorns, bay leaf and mace to the milk; bring very slowly to the boil then strain and use to make the sauce.

With wet hands form the meat mixture into about sixteen small balls. Heat the oil and fry the meatballs for 4 minutes. Drain on absorbent paper.

Place the drained meatballs in a serving dish and pour over the mustard sauce. If liked any extra sauce can be served separately in a sauce boat.

Meatballs in mustard sauce*

IMPERIAL	AMERICAN
½ carrot	½ carrot
1 small onion	1 small onion
1 pint milk	2½ cups milk
1 bay leaf	1 bay leaf
2 peppercorns	2 peppercorns
good pinch mace	good pinch mace
2 oz. butter	¼ cup butter
2 oz. flour	½ cup all-purpose flour
1 tablespoon dry mustard	1 tablespoon dry mustard
1 tablespoon vinegar	1 tablespoon vinegar
salt and pepper to taste	salt and pepper to taste
2 slices stale bread	2 slices stale bread
1 lb. lean beef	1 lb. lean beef
2 oz. bacon	3 bacon slices
2 tablespoons chopped parsley	3 tablespoons chopped parsley
1 teaspoon salt	1 teaspoon salt
½ teaspoon dry mustard	½ teaspoon dry mustard
2 eggs	2 eggs
oil for frying	oil for frying

Peel and roughly slice the carrot and half the onion. Place in a saucepan with the milk, bay leaf, peppercorns and mace and bring very slowly to the boil. Allow to stand 10 minutes, then strain. Melt the butter, add flour and cook without browning for 5 minutes. Add the milk, mustard, vinegar and seasoning and bring to the boil, stirring all the time until sauce thickens. Keep hot. To make the meatballs, soak the bread in cold water for 5 minutes, squeeze dry and break up with a fork. Mince the beef, bacon and remaining onion together, mix with the bread, seasonings and eggs. With wet hands, shape the mixture into about sixteen small balls. Heat the oil and fry the meatballs in deep heated oil for 4 minutes. Drain and serve with the sauce poured over.

* To freeze, pack meatballs and sauce separately.

Stewed oxtail

IMPERIAL	AMERICAN
1 oxtail, cut into joints	1 oxtail, cut into joints
1 oz. seasoned flour	¼ cup seasoned flour
2 tablespoons oil	3 tablespoons oil
1 onion, sliced	1 onion, sliced
1 carrot, sliced	1 carrot, sliced
1 turnip, sliced	1 turnip, sliced
1 stick celery, sliced	1 stalk celery, sliced
2 tablespoons tomato purée	3 tablespoons tomato paste
1 pint beef stock	2½ cups beef stock
bouquet garni	bouquet garni
salt and pepper to taste	salt and pepper to taste

Wipe the meat and coat well in the seasoned flour. Heat the oil in a heavy pan and brown the meat on all sides. Sprinkle any remaining flour over the meat and cook slightly until beginning to brown then add the vegetables and tomato purée. Add the stock and bring to the boil, stirring constantly then add the bouquet garni and seasoning. Simmer, covered tightly for 2–2½ hours until the meat is almost falling from the bones.

Ilchester beef cobbler

IMPERIAL	AMERICAN
2 lb. shin of beef, cut in 1-inch pieces	2 lb. boneless shank knuckle, in 1-inch pieces
2 oz. flour	½ cup all-purpose flour
salt and pepper	salt and pepper
2 tablespoons cooking oil	3 tablespoons cooking oil
1 lb. leeks, sliced	1 lb. leeks, sliced
1 small head celery, cut in 1-inch pieces	1 small bunch celery, cut in 1-inch pieces
8 oz. carrots, sliced	½ lb. carrots, sliced
½ pint beer	1¼ cups light beer
½ pint beef stock	1¼ cups beef stock
Topping:	Topping:
8 oz. self-raising flour	2 cups all-purpose flour sifted with 2¼ teaspoons baking powder
½ teaspoon salt	½ teaspoon salt
1 oz. butter	2 tablespoons butter
1½ teaspoons dried basil	1½ teaspoons dried basil
1½ oz. grated Parmesan and 1½ oz. Cheddar cheese, mixed	3 tablespoons grated Parmesan and 3 tablespoons Cheddar cheese, mixed
¼ pint milk	⅔ cup milk

Toss meat in seasoned flour. Heat oil in frying pan, add meat and fry until brown on all sides. Add vegetables and cook for a further 2–3 minutes. Stir in any remaining flour from the meat. Pour in beer and stock and bring to the boil. Transfer to a 3-pint casserole, cover and cook in a moderate oven, 350°F, 180°C, Gas Mark 4, for about 1½–2 hours until meat is tender.
To make the topping, mix flour and salt together and rub in butter. Mix in herbs and half the cheese. About 30 minutes before serving casserole, increase oven temperature to 375°F, 190°C, Gas Mark 5. Finish making topping by binding flour and cheese mixture together with milk. Roll out on a floured surface to ½-inch thickness and cut into rounds with a 1½-inch plain cutter. Remove cover from casserole and adjust seasoning. Arrange scone rounds overlapping on top. Sprinkle tops with remaining cheese. Return to oven and bake for about 15 minutes until scone topping is golden. Serve at once. (*Serves 6.*)

Lamb chain with economy cuts

The breast, scrag end and middle neck from a lamb weighing about 30 lb. will give about 4½ lb. boned meat which will produce sufficient basic stew to make three meals for six people. Different vegetables can be added when the stew is served.

Basic lamb stew*

IMPERIAL	AMERICAN
2 breasts, scrag end and middle neck from 1 whole lamb	2 breasts and 1 shoulder from 1 whole lamb
2 tablespoons dried onion flakes	3 tablespoons dried onion flakes
3 teaspoons salt	3 teaspoons salt
1 teaspoon pepper	1 teaspoon pepper
½ lemon	½ lemon

Put all the ingredients into a large pan, or into two saucepans, add enough water to cover, bring to the boil slowly. Skim, cover and simmer for 1–1½ hours, or until meat can easily be removed from bones. Allow to cool until surplus fat can be skimmed from the surface, but has not completely set. Remove as many of the bones as possible, washing your hands carefully before touching the meat. Reduce the remaining stock by half and freeze the meat in three suitable containers with the stock.

1 Lamb printanière

IMPERIAL	AMERICAN
1 oz. butter	2 tablespoons butter
1 clove garlic, crushed	1 clove garlic, crushed
8 oz. diced frozen carrots or mixed vegetables	½ lb. diced frozen carrots or mixed vegetables
½ teaspoon dried mixed sweet herbs	½ teaspoon dried mixed sweet herbs
1 tablespoon tomato purée	1 tablespoon tomato paste
8 oz. frozen peas	½ lb. frozen peas
8 oz. cooked new potatoes	½ lb. cooked new potatoes
1 container basic lamb stew, defrosted	1 container basic lamb stew, defrosted

Melt the butter in a large saucepan, toss the garlic and carrots in the covered pan for 1–2 minutes, add the herbs and tomato purée dissolved in 2 tablespoons (U.S. 3 tablespoons) hot water, the peas and potatoes. Cover the pan and simmer gently until all the vegetables are cooked, about 5 minutes. Stir in the stewed lamb, reheat until it comes to the boil and serve garnished with fried bread croûtons. (*Serves 6.*)

2 Lamb with haricot beans

IMPERIAL	AMERICAN
8 oz. haricot beans	½ lb. navy beans
2 oz. dripping	¼ cup drippings
1 large onion, chopped	1 large onion, chopped
1 container basic lamb stew, defrosted	1 container basic lamb stew, defrosted
2 tablespoons diced garlic sausage	3 tablespoons diced garlic sausage
2 tablespoons chopped parsley	3 tablespoons chopped parsley
salt and pepper to taste	salt and pepper to taste

Soak the beans overnight in sufficient water to cover. Next day, drain and put beans in a large saucepan with the dripping, onion and sufficient fresh water to cover. Simmer for about 1½ hours or until beans are almost cooked. Add the stewed lamb, garlic sausage and parsley and reheat until it comes to the boil, taste, adding more salt and pepper if necessary. (*Serves 6.*)

3 Greek lamb stew

IMPERIAL	AMERICAN
8 oz. mushrooms, sliced	½ lb. mushrooms, sliced
1 tablespoon corn oil	1 tablespoon corn oil
1 lemon	1 lemon
1 container basic lamb stew, defrosted	1 container basic lamb stew, defrosted
1 5-oz. carton natural yogurt	⅔ cup natural yogurt

Toss the mushrooms in the heated corn oil until they begin to change colour. Then add the juice of the lemon and 1 teaspoon grated lemon zest. Cover the pan and simmer for 5 minutes or until the mushrooms are cooked. Add the stewed lamb, reheat and gradually stir in the yogurt. Taste and add more salt and pepper if necessary. (*Serves 6.*)

Irish stew

IMPERIAL	AMERICAN
2 lb. neck of lamb, in neat pieces	2 lb. lamb neck slices
2 lb. potatoes, sliced	2 lb. potatoes, sliced
2 large onions, sliced	2 large onions, sliced
2 carrots, sliced	2 carrots, sliced
salt and pepper to taste	salt and pepper to taste

Arrange meat and vegetables in layers in a deep flameproof casserole. Sprinkle each layer with salt and pepper and end with a layer of potatoes. Add water almost to cover, bring to the boil, cover and simmer for 2 hours, or cook in a very moderate oven, 325°F, 170°C, Gas Mark 3, for 2 hours, removing the lid for the last 20 minutes if you like a crisp potato topping. Traditionally served with pickled red cabbage.

Madras curry*

IMPERIAL	AMERICAN
1 lb. boned shoulder of lamb	1 lb. boneless lamb shoulder
salt and pepper to taste	salt and pepper to taste
4 onions	4 onions
1 teaspoon brown sugar	1 teaspoon brown sugar
2 tablespoons curry powder	3 tablespoons curry powder
large pinch ground ginger	large pinch ground ginger
1 lemon	1 lemon
2 chicken stock cubes	2 chicken bouillon cubes
1 oz. toasted blanched almonds	scant ½ cup toasted blanched almonds

Cut lamb into neat pieces and sprinkle with salt and pepper. Fry meat, peeled and sliced onions, sugar, curry powder and ginger in a large saucepan for 5 minutes. Add grated zest and juice of the lemon and the stock cubes. Cover with cold water, bring slowly to the boil, cover and simmer for 2 hours. Serve the curry garnished with the toasted almonds.

* Remember that the spices intensify in flavour after a few weeks in the freezer so unless a very strong curry is liked, decrease quantity of curry powder slightly.

Moussaka

IMPERIAL	AMERICAN
1 medium-sized onion	1 medium-sized onion
3 tablespoons oil	scant ¼ cup oil
1 lb. cooked lamb	1 lb. cooked lamb
2 tablespoons tomato purée	3 tablespoons tomato paste
seasoning to taste	seasoning to taste
1 large aubergine	1 large eggplant
8 oz. tomatoes or 1 8-oz. can	½ lb. tomatoes or 1 8-oz. can
8 oz. potatoes	½ lb. potatoes
1 egg yolk	1 egg yolk
½ pint cheese sauce	1¼ cups cheese sauce
2 oz. Cheddar or Parmesan cheese, grated	½ cup grated Cheddar or Parmesan cheese

Peel and slice the onion and sauté in 1 tablespoon of the oil. Add the meat cut into neat dice and toss well over high heat for 2 minutes. Add tomato purée and seasoning, and put in an ovenproof casserole. Heat another tablespoon of oil, cook the sliced aubergine for 5 minutes, turning once then arrange on top of the meat. Slice the tomatoes and place on top of the aubergines. Peel and slice the potatoes and fry in the remaining oil until beginning to brown then place on top of the tomatoes in the casserole. Add the egg yolk to the prepared cheese sauce and pour over the dish, sprinkle the top with grated cheese and bake in a moderate oven, 350°F, 180°C, Gas Mark 4, for 20–25 minutes until well browned.

Crunchy lamb rissoles*

IMPERIAL	AMERICAN
1 lb. cooked lamb	1 lb. cooked lamb
2 oz. corn flakes	2 cups corn flakes
½ teaspoon mixed herbs	½ teaspoon mixed herbs
1 tablespoon flour	1 tablespoon all-purpose flour
salt and pepper to taste	salt and pepper to taste
2 tablespoons tomato ketchup	3 tablespoons tomato catsup
1 teaspoon Worcestershire sauce	1 teaspoon Worcestershire sauce
2 eggs	2 eggs
Coating:	*Coating:*
1 egg	1 egg
2 oz. corn flakes	2 cups corn flakes
oil for frying	oil for frying

Mince the lamb and mix together with the crushed corn flakes, herbs, flour and seasoning. Combine tomato ketchup, Worcestershire sauce and eggs and use to bind the mixture together. Shape into eight rissoles. Coat each rissole in beaten egg and then in crushed corn flakes and fry gently in shallow oil for about 3 minutes on each side. Drain on absorbent paper and serve hot or cold.

* To freeze, pack cooked in layers in a rigid-based container with dividers.

Pork and ham risotto

IMPERIAL	AMERICAN
1 medium-sized onion, chopped	1 medium-sized onion, chopped
8 oz. long-grain rice	generous 1 cup long-grain rice
2 tablespoons oil	3 tablespoons oil
1½ pints chicken stock	3¾ cups chicken stock
4 large tomatoes, chopped	4 large tomatoes, chopped
8 oz. cooked pork, diced	½ lb. cooked pork, diced
2 oz. ham, diced	¼ cup diced cooked ham
salt and pepper to taste	salt and pepper to taste

Fry onion and rice gently in the oil for 3 minutes. Stir in stock, chopped tomatoes, meats and seasoning. Cover and simmer for 20 minutes, or until stock is absorbed. Serve with a cucumber salad.

Mix the minced lamb with the crushed corn flakes, herbs, flour and seasoning. Bind together with the tomato ketchup mixture.

Dip the shaped rissoles in beaten egg and then coat them in crushed corn flakes. Fry gently in heated shallow oil for about 3 minutes on each side.

Drain the cooked rissoles on absorbent paper. Serve either hot or cold. To freeze, pack cooked in layers in a rigid based container with dividers.

Boned and rolled breast of lamb needs a well-seasoned stuffing to absorb the fat from the joint. This one is made from breadcrumbs, egg, corn kernels, onion and thyme.

Roast stuffed breast of lamb should be sliced across the end of the roll so that each serving includes a good proportion of stuffing.

Boned breast of lamb makes a tasty stew if well flavoured with vegetables and herbs. Surplus fat should be skimmed off part way through cooking.

Breast of lamb with thyme stuffing

IMPERIAL	AMERICAN
1 oz. butter	2 tablespoons butter
1 small onion, chopped	1 small onion, chopped
1 12-oz. can corn kernels, drained	1 12-oz. can kernel corn, drained
3 oz. fresh white breadcrumbs	1½ cups fresh soft bread crumbs
1 teaspoon lemon thyme, or thyme (dried), or 2 teaspoons fresh herbs	1 teaspoon lemon thyme, or thyme (dried), or 2 teaspoon fresh herbs
squeeze lemon juice	squeeze lemon juice
salt and pepper	salt and pepper
1 egg, lightly beaten	1 egg, lightly beaten
1 breast of lamb, boned	1 boneless breast of lamb

Melt the butter in a pan, and fry the onion gently until softened but not coloured. Remove from heat, stir in the well-drained corn kernels, breadcrumbs, herbs, lemon juice and seasoning. Bind with the egg and use to stuff the breast of lamb. Tie (or secure with wooden skewers) sufficiently loosely to allow for expansion of the stuffing, and roast for 40 minutes per pound (weigh the joint when stuffed), in a moderate oven, 350°F, 180°C, Gas Mark 4.

Navarin of lamb

IMPERIAL	AMERICAN
1 small breast of lamb, boned and cubed	1 small boneless breast of lamb, cubed
1 oz. seasoned flour	¼ cup seasoned flour
¾ pint stock	scant 2 cups stock
4 medium-sized onions, chopped	4 medium-sized onions, chopped
4 sticks celery, chopped	4 stalks celery, chopped
½ teaspoon dried mixed herbs	½ teaspoon dried mixed herbs
2 medium-sized carrots, sliced	2 medium-sized carrots, sliced
8 oz. small potatoes	½ lb. small potatoes
salt and pepper to taste	salt and pepper to taste
1 tablespoon chopped parsley	1 tablespoon chopped parsley

Trim surplus fat off meat cubes, place in a flameproof casserole over low heat until fat runs; remove. Toss the meat in the seasoned flour, add to pan and sauté gently until lightly browned. Add the stock, bring to the boil, add the onions, celery, herbs and carrots. Cover and simmer for 1 hour, skim off surplus fat, add the potatoes and continue cooking, covered, until meat and potatoes are tender. Taste and adjust seasoning if necessary; serve sprinkled with chopped parsley. Traditionally served with French bread.

Automatic oven menu (1)

Lemon lamb casserole
Baked potatoes with soured cream and chive dressing
Stuffed baked apples

IMPERIAL	AMERICAN
1½ lb. lamb cutlets	1½ lb. lamb rib chops
1 lb. parsnips, par-boiled and sliced	1 lb. parsnips, par-boiled and sliced
1 large onion, sliced	1 large onion, sliced
4 oz. dried apricots, soaked overnight	scant 1 cup dried apricots, soaked overnight
salt and black pepper to taste	salt and black pepper to taste
1 clove garlic, crushed	1 clove garlic, crushed
pinch dried rosemary	pinch dried rosemary
zest and juice 1 lemon	zest and juice 1 lemon
2 tomatoes, skinned and sliced	2 tomatoes, skinned and sliced
½ pint stock	1¼ cups stock

Place the cutlets in a medium-sized ovenproof casserole with the parsnips, onion and drained apricots. Season well with salt and black pepper between each layer and add the garlic, rosemary and grated zest. Finish with a layer of tomato slices. Pour lemon juice over casserole and add sufficient stock to just cover meat. Cover tightly and place in centre of oven. Take 4 medium-sized potatoes, clean well and score a line round the centre of each. Put on a baking sheet and place on top shelf of oven. Wash and core 4 medium-sized cooking apples. Mix together 3 tablespoons fruit mincemeat, the grated zest of 1 lemon, 2 oz. (U.S. ½ cup) chopped walnuts and 2 teaspoons Angostura bitters. Place the apples on a baking sheet, fill the centres with the stuffing and pour 1 teaspoon of golden syrup over each apple. Put the tray in bottom of oven.

Preset the oven at moderate, 350°F, 180°C, Gas Mark 4, to start cooking 1½ hours before you will be ready to eat.

Just before serving, prepare dressing for potatoes by whisking a few finely chopped chives into a 5-oz. (U.S. ⅔ cup) carton of soured cream. When removing meat from oven, place tray of apples if necessary, on top shelf for a further few minutes.

Automatic oven menu (2)

Roast lamb with rosemary and garlic
Roast potatoes
Braised celery
Rice Josephine

Take a 3–4 lb. leg of lamb and score skin on rounded side diagonally. Place a ¼ clove of garlic in each cross cut (using 3–4 cloves in all) and sprinkle dried rosemary over the surface. Place in a roasting pan with 4 tablespoons (U.S. ⅓ cup) water, cover with a piece of foil and place on centre shelf of oven. Cut 4 medium-sized potatoes into even pieces and completely coat with melted lard. Put in roasting pan and place on top shelf of oven. Clean and chop 1 large head of celery and place in a casserole with enough water to cover and 1 teaspoon vegetable extract. Place on centre shelf with joint. Wash 2–3 oz. (U.S. about ¼ cup) round-grain rice and put into a greased ovenproof dish with 1 oz. (U.S. 2 tablespoons) sugar. Separate 2 eggs and beat the yolks into 1 pint (U.S. 2½ cups) milk. Pour over the rice, then stir in 2 tablespoons (U.S. 3 tablespoons) chopped mixed candied peel. Place in bottom of oven, in a bain-marie.

Preset oven at moderately hot, 375°F, 190°C, Gas Mark 5, to start cooking 1¾–2 hours before you will be ready to eat.

Remove the meat from the oven and keep warm. Make a meringue with 2 oz. (U.S. ¼ cup granulated) castor sugar and the 2 egg whites. Spread over rice pudding, raise oven heat slightly and place on top shelf in oven until meringue is golden.

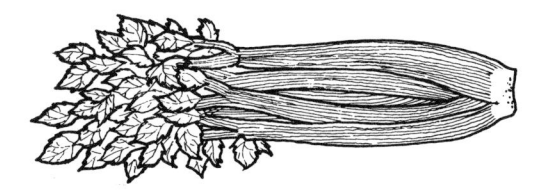

Roast belly pork in lemon and honey sauce

IMPERIAL	AMERICAN
2½–3 lb. joint belly pork	2½–3 lb. piece fresh picnic shoulder
1 tablespoon clear honey	1 tablespoon clear honey
juice and grated zest 2 lemons	juice and grated zest 2 lemons
2 teaspoons gravy powder	2 teaspoons gravy mix
½ pint water	1¼ cups water

Score, roll and tie the joint into a neat shape. Sprinkle with salt. Roast in a moderate oven, 350°F, 180°C, Gas Mark 4, for 35 minutes per pound and 35 minutes over. Remove joint on to a warm serving dish, skim surplus fat from the roasting pan, stir in the honey, lemon juice and zest. Moisten the gravy powder with a little of the water, add the rest of the water to the roasting pan and stir well. Bring the juices from the pan to the boil in a small saucepan, stir in the gravy mix and cook, stirring, over low heat until thick and smooth. If a crisp crackling is not required, brush the skin of the joint with a little extra clear honey 30 minutes before end of cooking time. (*Serves 6.*)

Saucy spare ribs*

IMPERIAL	AMERICAN
4 spare rib chops	4 sparerib chops
salt and pepper to taste	salt and pepper to taste
Sauce:	Sauce:
2 oz. butter	¼ cup butter
1 tablespoon flour	1 tablespoon all-purpose flour
large pinch dry mustard	large pinch dry mustard
large pinch paprika pepper	large pinch paprika pepper
1 tablespoon tomato purée	1 tablespoon tomato paste
1 tablespoon vinegar	1 tablespoon vinegar
1 tablespoon Worcestershire sauce	1 tablespoon Worcestershire sauce
¾ pint chicken stock	scant 2 cups chicken stock
1 orange	1 orange

Wipe and trim the chops. Sprinkle with salt and pepper and grill or bake them for 30 minutes. Melt the butter in a large pan, add the flour, mustard and paprika pepper. Mix well then add the tomato purée, vinegar and Worcestershire sauce; bring to the boil and simmer for 2–3 minutes. Add the stock and reheat, stirring until thickened. Arrange chops on a serving dish and pour the sauce over. Peel the orange and cut into wedges, use to garnish the finished dish.

* To freeze, turn into a shaped foil dish and cover. Defrost and reheat in a hot oven, 425°F, 220°C, Gas Mark 7, for 40 minutes. Garnish with orange wedges as suggested above.

Country pork casserole

IMPERIAL	AMERICAN
1 lb. hand of pork	1 lb. fresh picnic shoulder
1½ oz. seasoned flour	generous ¼ cup seasoned flour
1 tablespoon oil	1 tablespoon oil
8 oz. leeks	½ lb. leeks
½ pint strong ale	1¼ cups strong ale
dash Tabasco sauce	dash Tabasco sauce
bouquet garni	bouquet garni
salt and pepper to taste	salt and pepper to taste

Bone the pork and cut into 1-inch pieces. Toss in the flour and sauté in the hot oil until browned. Clean and chop the leeks, add to the pork and toss to brown for a few minutes. Stir in the remaining flour, the ale and Tabasco sauce. Bring to the boil, stirring until thickened. Add the bouquet garni and salt and pepper. Cover and simmer over low heat for 1¼–1½ hours, stirring occasionally. Remove bouquet garni, check seasoning and serve with creamed potatoes, and buttered vegetables.

Sweet and sour pork

IMPERIAL	AMERICAN
1 lb. boned belly of pork	1 lb. boneless fresh picnic shoulder
salt and pepper to taste	salt and pepper to taste
Sauce:	Sauce:
1 small onion	1 small onion
2 oz. butter	¼ cup butter
2 tablespoons brown sugar	3 tablespoons brown sugar
3 tablespoons vinegar	scant ¼ cup vinegar
1 pint chicken stock	2½ cups chicken stock
1 3¼-oz. can pimentos	1 3¼-oz. can pimientos
1 tablespoon flour	1 tablespoon all-purpose flour
1 teaspoon dry mustard	1 teaspoon dry mustard
Batter:	Batter:
4 oz. self-raising flour	1 cup all-purpose flour sifted with 1 teaspoon baking powder
large pinch salt	large pinch salt
1 tablespoon oil	1 tablespoon oil
5 tablespoons water	6 tablespoons water
1 egg white	1 egg white
oil for deep frying	oil for deep frying

De-rind the pork and cut into 1-inch cubes. Sprinkle with salt and pepper and fry slowly in a dry frying pan until fat runs, then fry briskly until golden brown. Peel and chop the onion and fry in the butter until softened. Add the sugar, vinegar and stock and bring to the boil. Simmer for 5 minutes. Drain the pimentos, cut into strips and add to the pan. Blend flour and mustard with a little water, stir into the pan and bring to the boil. To make the batter, mix together the flour, salt and oil then gradually beat in the measured water. Whisk the egg white stiffly and fold in then dip the pork cubes into the batter and fry in deep oil until golden brown. Drain and serve the pork on a bed of noodles with the sauce poured over.

Piquant pork stew with parsley and lemon dumplings*

IMPERIAL	AMERICAN
1 oz. shredded suet	scant ¼ cup finely chopped suet
1 lb. lean blade bone of pork, cubed	1 lb. pork stew meat, diced
2 onions, sliced	2 onions, sliced
1 tablespoon plain flour	1 tablespoon all-purpose flour
1 pint chicken stock	2½ cups chicken stock
1 bay leaf	1 bay leaf
pinch salt and pepper	pinch salt and pepper
4 oz. prunes	¼ lb. prunes

Dumplings:
4 oz. self-raising flour

2 oz. shredded suet

pinch salt and pepper
1 tablespoon chopped parsley
grated zest and juice 1 lemon

Dumplings:
1 cup all-purpose flour sifted with 1 teaspoon baking powder
scant ½ cup finely chopped suet
pinch salt and pepper
1 tablespoon chopped parsley
grated zest and juice 1 lemon

Melt suet and use to fry pork and onions for a few minutes. Stir in the flour and cook for 1 minute. Gradually blend in the stock, add bay leaf, seasoning and prunes and bring to the boil, stirring constantly. Cover pan and simmer for 1 hour. Mix together the dumpling ingredients with sufficient water to make a firm dough. Divide into eight, shape into balls with floured hands and if serving immediately place on top of stew. Cover pan and simmer for a further 20 minutes.

* To freeze, pack stew in a plastic container and freeze the uncooked dumplings separately. To serve, allow stew to defrost. Place in saucepan and reheat then place dumplings on top and simmer for a further 20 minutes.

Liver and apple hot-pot

IMPERIAL	AMERICAN
1 lb. lamb's liver	1 lb. lamb liver
1 tablespoon corn oil	1 tablespoon corn oil
½ oz. butter	1 tablespoon butter
1 medium-sized onion	1 medium-sized onion
2 large carrots	2 large carrots
2 sticks celery	2 stalks celery
1 green pepper	1 green sweet pepper
2 medium-sized cooking apples	2 medium-sized baking apples
salt to taste	salt to taste
freshly ground black pepper	freshly ground black pepper
½ pint stock, slightly thickened	1¼ cups stock, slightly thickened
1 lb. potatoes	1 lb. potatoes
1 oz. butter	2 tablespoons butter

Slice the liver and sauté for 1 minute on each side in the hot oil and butter. Peel and slice onion and carrots, slice celery, de-seed and slice the green pepper, peel, core and slice the apples. Layer the liver alternately with these vegetables and seasonings in an ovenproof dish. Pour in the stock. Peel and thinly slice the potatoes and arrange on top of the casserole in concentric circles. Melt the butter and brush the potatoes liberally. Bake in a moderately hot oven, 375°F, 190°C, Gas Mark 5, for 1 hour.

Sauté the sliced liver for 1 minute on each side, then place in alternate layers with the prepared vegetables in an ovenproof dish.

Arrange the thinly sliced potatoes on top of the casserole in concentric circles. Brush the potatoes with melted butter before putting in the oven.

Bake the liver and apple hot-pot in a moderately hot oven for 1 hour. Serve from the ovenproof dish. If liked serve with a tossed green salad.

Braised liver and bacon

IMPERIAL	AMERICAN
1 lb. ox liver, sliced	1 lb. beef liver, sliced
seasoned flour	seasoned flour
2 tablespoons oil	3 tablespoons oil
1 onion, sliced	1 onion, sliced
1 carrot, sliced	1 carrot, sliced
8 oz. streaky bacon	½ lb. bacon slices
salt and pepper to taste	salt and pepper to taste
½ pint beef stock	1¼ cups beef stock

Wash the liver, pat dry and coat in the seasoned flour. Heat the oil and sauté the liver to brown. Add the onion and carrot, brown slightly then add the remaining seasoned flour. Place liver and vegetables in the casserole in layers with the bacon, season well and pour in the stock. Cover and cook in a moderately hot oven, 375°F, 190°C, Gas Mark 5, for 1 hour.
Note: Pig's liver can be substituted for ox liver.

Stuffed ox heart

IMPERIAL	AMERICAN
1 ox heart	1 beef heart
4 oz. onion and mushroom stuffing, see page 71	1 cup onion and mushroom stuffing, see page 71
dripping	drippings
salt and pepper to taste	salt and pepper to taste
4 rashers streaky bacon	4 bacon slices

Soak the trimmed heart in cold water for 2–3 hours, drain and dry. Stuff the heart and sew up with white cotton. Wrap tightly in foil, place in a saucepan and cover with cold water. Bring to the boil and simmer for 2 hours. Remove the heart from the pan, take off foil and place heart in a roasting pan. Brush with dripping, season and wrap with bacon rashers. Roast in a moderately hot oven, 375°F, 190°C, Gas Mark 5, for 1 hour, basting frequently.

Guernsey creamed tripe

IMPERIAL	AMERICAN
2 lb. tripe	2 lb. tripe
2 oz. dripping	¼ cup drippings
2 medium-sized onions, finely chopped	2 medium-sized onions, finely chopped
2 tablespoons chopped fresh herbs	3 tablespoons chopped fresh herbs
1 tablespoon flour	1 tablespoon flour
1 lb. tomatoes, skinned and chopped	1 lb. tomatoes, skinned and chopped
salt and pepper to taste	salt and pepper to taste
2 tablespoons single cream	3 tablespoons coffee cream

Cut the tripe into fairly wide strips and blanch by plunging it into boiling water for 2 minutes. Melt the dripping in a flameproof casserole and fry the onions gently until golden. Add the chopped herbs and fry for a further 3 minutes. Stir in the flour and cook over gentle heat without browning for 2 minutes then add the sieved tomato pulp. Bring to the boil, stirring constantly until the mixture bubbles then add the tripe, season to taste, cover and simmer for 1½ hours. Remove from the heat and stir in the cream.

Faggots

IMPERIAL	AMERICAN
1 lb. pig's liver, minced	1 lb. pork liver, ground
10 oz. fat belly of pork, minced	1¼ cups ground fresh picnic shoulder
2 medium-sized onions, chopped	2 medium-sized onions, chopped
½ teaspoon dried sage	½ teaspoon dried sage
salt and pepper to taste	salt and pepper to taste
½ teaspoon powdered mace	½ teaspoon powdered mace
4 oz. fresh white breadcrumbs	2 cups fresh soft bread crumbs
1 large egg, beaten	1 egg, beaten
large piece of caul, in 3-inch squares or 6-inch squares cooking film	6-inch squares cooking film
little stock or gravy	little stock or gravy

Mix together the liver and pork and place in a frying pan with the onions, sage and seasoning. Cook gently for about 30 minutes then drain and reserve juice. Place meat in a basin with the mace, breadcrumbs and make a stiff mixture with the egg. Adjust seasoning and form the mixture into ten balls and wrap each one in squares of caul which have been soaked for 1 hour in warm water and a dash of vinegar (or use cooking film). Pack faggots into a greased baking dish, pour stock round and cook in a moderate oven, 350°F, 180°C, Gas Mark 4, for 1 hour. Drain off juice again, add to reserved juice, skim and pour round the faggots 5 minutes before serving.
Note: Caul is a type of fatty membrane which forms part of a pig's or sheep's intestine. Your butcher should be able to supply this on request.

Cooking for company

It is a great boost to your morale to spend a little more on the ingredients now and again, and present a luxurious meal when entertaining your friends. Even then the cost need not be excessive if your repertoire includes some unusual dishes such as stuffed lamb shoulder with apricot cups or curried mince with watercress salad.

Roulades de veau

(Illustrated in colour on page 19)

IMPERIAL	AMERICAN
4 portions veal fillet	4 veal scallops
Filling:	Filling:
½ teaspoon Tabasco sauce	½ teaspoon Tabasco sauce
1 egg	1 egg
2 oz. fresh white breadcrumbs	1 cup fresh soft bread crumbs
1 tablespoon grated Parmesan cheese	1 tablespoon grated Parmesan cheese
2 tablespoons chopped parsley	3 tablespoons chopped parsley
1 teaspoon salt	1 teaspoon salt
Sauce:	Sauce:
2 teaspoons paprika pepper	2 teaspoons paprika pepper
2 teaspoons flour	2 teaspoons all-purpose flour
1 tablespoon oil	1 tablespoon oil
1 oz. butter	2 tablespoons butter
1 15½-oz. can tomato juice	1 15½-oz. can tomato juice
1 lb. mashed potato	1 lb. mashed potato
chopped parsley to garnish	chopped parsley to garnish

Put veal fillets between two thicknesses of greaseproof paper and beat out thinly. Mix together the Tabasco, egg and other filling ingredients and spread over the fillets. Roll up tightly and wrap each portion closely in foil or greaseproof paper and secure. Chill for about 1 hour. When ready to cook, remove the wrapping and if necessary tie each roll with strong white thread but this may not be needed. Mix the paprika pepper and flour together and use some to coat the rolls, patting on gently. Brown them lightly in the hot oil and butter mixture in a small flameproof casserole. Turn once, packing rolls as closely together as possible. Add the tomato juice to cover the rolls, cover casserole and simmer until the rolls are tender, about 30 minutes. Blend rest of flour and paprika mixture with a little cold water, pour some of the sauce from the casserole into this and blend smoothly. Add to the casserole, boil for 3 minutes. Remove thread (if used) from rolls. Pipe a border of mashed potato round a hot serving dish, arrange the rolls in the centre and spoon some sauce over them. Sprinkle with chopped parsley. Hand rest of sauce separately.

Sweet Malayan veal*

IMPERIAL	AMERICAN
1 lb. lean veal	1 lb. lean veal
2 tablespoons seasoned flour	3 tablespoons seasoned flour
3 tablespoons corn oil	scant ¼ cup corn oil
4 small onions	4 small onions
4 oz. mushrooms	¼ lb. mushrooms
1 green pepper	1 green sweet pepper
1 8-oz. can pineapple chunks	1 8-oz. can pineapple chunks
2 firm tomatoes	2 firm tomatoes
1 tablespoon soya sauce	1 tablespoon soy sauce
2 tablespoons vinegar	3 tablespoons vinegar
1 tablespoon honey	1 tablespoon honey
salt and pepper to taste	salt and pepper to taste
1 tablespoon cornflour	1 tablespoon cornstarch

Cut the veal into 1-inch cubes, toss in the seasoned flour and sauté in the hot oil until browned on all sides. Peel and quarter the onions, slice the mushrooms and de-seed and slice the pepper. Add these to the pan and sauté, stirring frequently, for 3–5 minutes. Add the canned pineapple and juice, skinned and quartered tomatoes, soya sauce, vinegar, honey and salt and pepper to taste. Simmer for 5–10 minutes until the veal is tender. Blend the cornflour with a little water and add as much as required to slightly thicken the sauce. Simmer for a further 2–3 minutes then serve surrounded by a border of cooked rice.

* To freeze, put the veal with the sauce in a shaped foil dish and cover. Defrost and reheat in a hot oven, 425°F, 220°C, Gas Mark 7, for 40 minutes.

Veal flamenco

IMPERIAL	AMERICAN
4 veal chops	4 veal chops
1 tablespoon seasoned flour	1 tablespoon seasoned flour
3 tablespoons corn oil	scant ¼ cup corn oil
1 red or green pepper	1 red or green sweet pepper
1 large onion	1 large onion
1 8-oz. can tomatoes	1 8-oz. can tomatoes
¼ pint chicken stock	⅔ cup chicken stock
4 tablespoons single cream	⅓ cup coffee cream
1 tablespoon chopped parsley	1 tablespoon chopped parsley

Coat the chops in the seasoned flour and fry in the hot oil until browned on both sides. Remove, drain and keep hot. Chop the pepper, peel and chop the onion and add both to the pan. Sauté until golden brown. Add the remaining flour, stir well and add the tomatoes and chicken stock. Replace the chops, cover and simmer for 20–30 minutes, until the chops are tender. Stir in the cream, heat without boiling. Serve immediately, sprinkled with chopped parsley and accompanied by fluffy rice.

Escalopes de veau meunière

IMPERIAL	AMERICAN
4 thin slices fillet of veal	4 veal scallops
1 tablespoon seasoned flour	1 tablespoon seasoned flour
2 oz. butter	¼ cup butter
2 tablespoons corn oil	3 tablespoons corn oil
juice ½ lemon	juice ½ lemon
1 tablespoon drained capers	1 tablespoon drained capers

Beat the veal fillets between two thicknesses of greaseproof paper. Coat lightly in the seasoned flour. Heat half the butter with the oil in a frying pan, and fry the veal gently on both sides until golden brown. Do not make the fat in the pan too hot or the veal will shrink. Transfer to a warm serving dish, add the rest of the butter and the lemon juice to the fat in the pan. Return to the heat, stir in the capers and cook for 1 minute, or until fat just begins to brown. Pour over the veal fillets and serve with creamy mashed potato.

Note: Veal cooked in this way can be served without the butter sauce and topped with a few asparagus spears or with chopped ham and grated cheese.

Pork chops with orange honey glaze*

(Illustrated in colour on the opposite page)

IMPERIAL	AMERICAN
4 pork chops	4 pork chops
1 tablespoon corn oil	1 tablespoon corn oil
2 teaspoons soya sauce	2 teaspoons soy sauce
2 tablespoons honey	3 tablespoons honey
1 chicken stock cube	1 chicken bouillon cube
1 tablespoon tomato purée	1 tablespoon tomato paste
1 orange	1 orange
saffron rice	saffron rice
parsley sprigs to garnish	parsley sprigs to garnish

Fry the pork chops gently on both sides in the oil until lightly browned. Add the soya sauce, honey and stock cube and tomato purée dissolved in ½ pint (U.S. 1¼ cups) boiling water. Finely pare zest of orange, squeeze juice and add both to the sauce. Cover pan, reduce heat and continue cooking for 20 minutes. Meanwhile cook the saffron rice, spread on a warm serving dish, arrange the chops on top and continue cooking the sauce until it has reduced to the consistency of a glaze. Pour the glaze over the chops and garnish with parsley sprigs.

* To freeze, pack cooked chops with sauce, and rice separately. Garnish with parsley when serving.

Beef chop suey

IMPERIAL	AMERICAN
1 lb. rump steak	1 lb. sirloin steak
2 tablespoons corn oil	3 tablespoons corn oil
¼ small firm cabbage	¼ small firm cabbage
1 large onion	1 large onion
2 carrots	2 carrots
4 oz. mushrooms	¼ lb. mushrooms
1 8-oz. can bean sprouts	1 8-oz. can bean sprouts
1-2 tablespoons soya sauce	2–3 tablespoons soy sauce
2 tablespoons water	3 tablespoons water
salt and pepper to taste	salt and pepper to taste

Cut the meat into thin strips and fry quickly in the oil over high heat, tossing frequently until browned and just cooked. Remove and keep hot. Chop the cabbage, peel and thinly slice the onion, peel the carrots and cut them into thin strips and slice the mushrooms. Fry these in the remaining oil, tossing frequently until browned and just beginning to soften. Add the drained bean sprouts, soya sauce and water and simmer for 2–3 minutes. Add the steak and check the seasoning. Additional soya sauce can be added at the table by each person. Serve immediately while the bean sprouts are crisp.

Pork chops with orange honey glaze

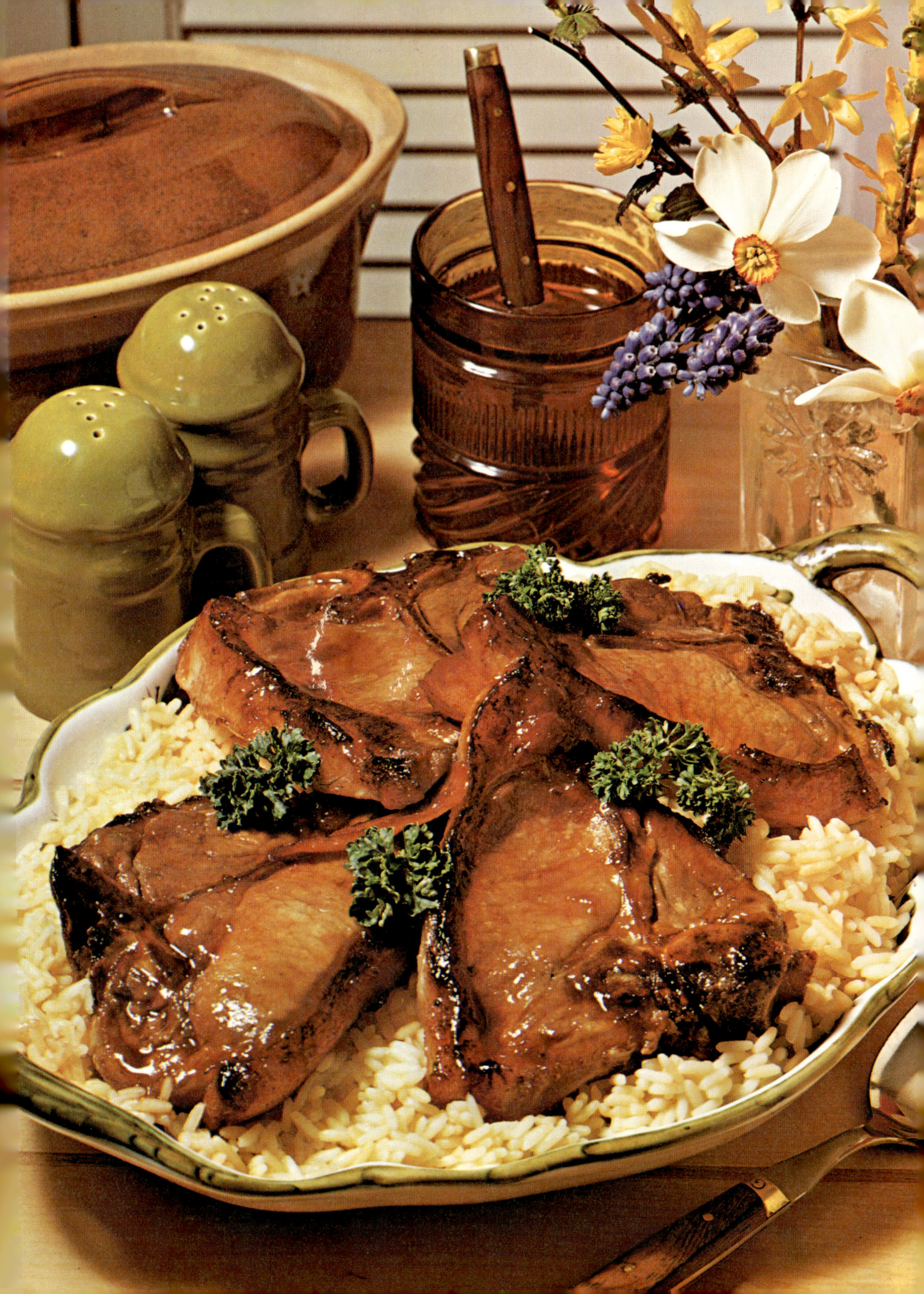

Cut the pork fillet into ½-inch slices. Melt the butter and cook the chopped onion for 3 minutes. Cook the rice in boiling salted water according to packet instructions.

Add the pork slices to the onions in the frying pan. Season with salt and pepper and cook for 10 minutes, turning once. Drain apricot halves.

Add the drained apricot halves to the pork and heat through. Pour the prepared sauce over and serve with a green salad.

Worcester fruited pork

IMPERIAL	AMERICAN
8 oz. quick-cook rice	generous 1 cup quick-cook rice
1 oz. butter	2 tablespoons butter
1 large onion, chopped	1 large onion, chopped
1 lb. pork fillet, in ½-inch slices	1 lb. pork tenderloin, in ½-inch slices
salt and pepper to taste	salt and pepper to taste
1 8-oz. can apricot halves	1 8-oz. can apricot halves
6 oz. brown sugar	¾ cup brown sugar
4 tablespoons apricot jam	⅓ cup apricot jam
4 tablespoons Worcestershire sauce	⅓ cup Worcestershire sauce
6 tablespoons vinegar	½ cup vinegar
1 teaspoon dry mustard	1 teaspoon dry mustard
1 teaspoon cornflour	1 teaspoon cornstarch

Measure water for rice, add salt and place pan over high heat. Melt the butter in a large frying pan, add onion and cook gently for 3 minutes. Add rice to boiling water and cook following packet instructions. Add pork to onions in the pan, season with salt and pepper and cook for 10 minutes, turning once. Drain the apricot halves, reserving syrup. Combine sugar, apricot jam, Worcestershire sauce, vinegar and mustard in a saucepan and heat gently to dissolve sugar. Moisten cornflour with a little apricot syrup and add remaining syrup to the sauce. Add apricot halves to pork and heat through. Bring sauce to the boil, stirring all the time until thickened. Place pork and apricots on serving dish, pour the sauce over and serve with boiled rice and a green salad.

Boeuf carbonnade*

IMPERIAL	AMERICAN
2 tablespoons oil	3 tablespoons oil
1 lb. chuck steak, in 1-inch cubes	1 lb. beef chuck, in 1-inch cubes
1 large onion, sliced	1 large onion, sliced
1 clove garlic, crushed	1 clove garlic, crushed
½ oz. flour	2 tablespoons all-purpose flour
salt and pepper to taste	salt and pepper to taste
bouquet garni	bouquet garni
½ pint brown ale or strong beer	1¼ cups dark beer
French bread	French bread
French mustard	French mustard

Heat the oil in a flameproof casserole, add the meat and brown all over. Add the onion and garlic and cook gently for 3 minutes. Sprinkle over the flour and stir well to brown slightly. Add the seasoning, bouquet garni, ale and a little water if necessary to cover the meat. Cook in a moderate oven, 325°F, 170°C, Gas Mark 3, for 1½ hours. If serving immediately cut enough slices of French bread to form a topping over the meat, spread each slice generously with French mustard and place mustard side up over the meat. Return to the oven for a further 15 minutes to crisp the bread.

* To freeze, pack in any suitable container without the bread. To serve, defrost and reheat. Add topping and place in a moderate oven for 15 minutes to crisp.

Daube marseillaise*

IMPERIAL	AMERICAN
1½ lb. topside beef, diced	1½ lb. beef round steak, diced
2 tablespoons olive oil	3 tablespoons olive oil
1 tablespoon flour	1 tablespoon all-purpose flour
¼ pint red wine	⅔ cup red wine
¼ pint water	⅔ cup water
2 cloves garlic (optional)	2 cloves garlic (optional)
bouquet garni	bouquet garni
2 teaspoons tomato purée	2 teaspoons tomato paste
salt and pepper to taste	salt and pepper to taste
3 oz. streaky bacon	4 bacon slices
12 button onions	12 button onions
4 oz. mushrooms	¼ lb. mushrooms
12 black olives	12 ripe olives

Brown the meat on all sides in the hot oil for 2–3 minutes. Sprinkle in the flour, stir until brown. Add the wine, water, crushed garlic, bouquet garni, tomato purée and seasoning. De-rind the bacon, chop and fry gently with the onions, mushrooms and olives. Add to the meat and cook in a daubière or tightly covered casserole in a low oven, 300°F, 150°C, Gas Mark 2 for about 3 hours. The meat should be so tender it can be cut with a spoon.

* To freeze, pack in any suitable container, defrost and reheat to serve.

Cold spiced beef

IMPERIAL	AMERICAN
2–3 lb. joint salt brisket	2–3 lb. piece uncooked corned beef
1 onion, sliced	1 onion, sliced
1 carrot, sliced	1 carrot, sliced
1 stick celery, sliced	1 stalk celery, sliced
6 peppercorns	6 peppercorns
6 cloves	6 cloves
¼ teaspoon mace	¼ teaspoon mace
2 bay leaves	2 bay leaves
few parsley sprigs	few parsley sprigs

Soak the beef in cold water overnight then drain and place in a saucepan. Cover with cold water, bring to the boil slowly and then drain off this liquid. Fill with fresh water, bring to the boil again and remove the grey scum which will form. Place the vegetables in the pan, together with all the spices. Bring to the boil and simmer for 2–3 hours until the meat is tender. Remove the meat and roll tightly to fit a deep 6–7-inch cake tin. Pour over a little strained stock from the pan, cover with a plate, place a weight on top and leave to cool. Place in the refrigerator or cold larder for 24 hours and served sliced with salads.

Note: As a buffet table centrepiece arrange a flower spray on top using thin strips of cucumber skin for stems and leaves and carrot slices for flowers. Coat with aspic jelly made from the strained stock and aspic crystals.

Curried mince with watercress salad

IMPERIAL	AMERICAN
1 large onion, chopped	1 large onion, chopped
2 oz. lard	¼ cup lard
1½–2 lb. lean minced beef	1½–2 lb. lean ground beef
1 tablespoon curry powder	1 tablespoon curry powder
1 oz. flour	¼ cup all-purpose flour
1 pint beef stock	2½ cups beef stock
1 tablespoon desiccated coconut	1 tablespoon shredded coconut
1 tablespoon boiling water	1 tablespoon boiling water
1 large cooking apple, diced	1 large baking apple, diced
salt and pepper to taste	salt and pepper to taste
Salad:	*Salad:*
1 lemon, sliced	1 lemon, sliced
3 eating apples, cored and sliced	3 dessert apples, cored and sliced
1 bunch watercress	1 bunch watercress
2 tablespoons lime juice	3 tablespoons lime juice

Fry onion gently in melted lard, add minced beef and cook, stirring until light brown. Add curry powder, cook 1–2 minutes, then stir in the flour. Gradually stir in the stock and bring to the boil. Scald coconut with boiling water, strain and add coconut milk and diced apple to curry. Season to taste and simmer for 30 minutes–1 hour.

To make the salad, arrange lemon and apple slices in a shallow dish, cover with watercress and sprinkle with lime juice. Toss just before serving. Serve curried mince with fluffy boiled rice, accompanied by the salad. (*Serves 6.*)

Steak, kidney and mushroom pie*

IMPERIAL	AMERICAN
1 oz. lard	2 tablespoons lard
1 lb. stewing steak, cubed	1 lb. beef stew meat, cubed
2 lamb's kidneys, cut into small pieces	2 lamb kidneys, cut into small pieces
1 onion, sliced	1 onion, sliced
1 tablespoon seasoned flour	1 tablespoon seasoned flour
½ pint dry red wine	1¼ cups dry red wine
¼ pint water	⅔ cup water
1 tablespoon tomato purée	1 tablespoon tomato paste
4 oz. mushrooms, sliced	¼ lb. mushrooms, sliced
Pastry:	Dough:
3 oz. shredded suet	generous ½ cup finely chopped suet
6 oz. self-raising flour	1½ cups all-purpose flour sifted with 1½ teaspoons baking powder
pinch salt and pepper	pinch salt and pepper
water to mix	water to mix

Melt lard and use to brown the steak, kidney and onion. Sprinkle on the flour and cook gently for 1 minute. Gradually blend in the wine and water and bring to the boil, stirring constantly. Add the tomato purée and mushrooms, cover pan and simmer for 1¼ hours. Allow to cool and transfer mixture to a shaped foil or ovenproof pie dish. To make the pastry, combine suet, flour and seasoning and add sufficient cold water to make a firm dough. Roll out and use to cover pie dish. Crimp the edges, make a small hole in the centre and brush with beaten egg or milk to glaze. Bake in a moderately hot oven, 400°F, 200°C, Gas Mark 6, for 30–35 minutes.

* To freeze, do not brush pastry with egg. Cool, cover and label. To serve, allow to defrost and then brush with beaten egg and bake as above.

Stuffed lamb shoulder with apricot cups

(Illustrated in colour on the opposite page)

IMPERIAL	AMERICAN
1 15-oz. can apricot halves	1 15-oz. can apricot halves
3 oz. fresh white breadcrumbs	1½ cups fresh soft bread crumbs
2 tablespoons chopped parsley	3 tablespoons chopped parsley
2 tablespoons lemon juice	3 tablespoons lemon juice
salt and pepper to taste	salt and pepper to taste
1 shoulder of lamb, boned	1 boneless lamb shoulder

Drain the apricot halves well, and chop half of them finely. Mix together the breadcrumbs, chopped apricots, parsley, lemon juice and seasoning with sufficient syrup from the can to make a firm consistency for the stuffing. Spread open the joint and use half the stuffing to fill the centre. Secure with two skewers, weigh and place, skewered side down, in a roasting pan. Pour a little more syrup and 2 tablespoons (U.S. 3 tablespoons) water round the joint. Roast according to the chart on page 9. With floured hands make up the rest of the stuffing mixture into balls. Place one stuffing ball in all but three of the apricot halves and bake round the joint for the last 45 minutes of cooking time, brushing well with fat from meat. Remove any surplus fat from the pan first, and brush the joint with more apricot syrup. Serve the joint on a hot dish surrounded by the apricot cups, and garnished with the reserved apricot halves, heated.

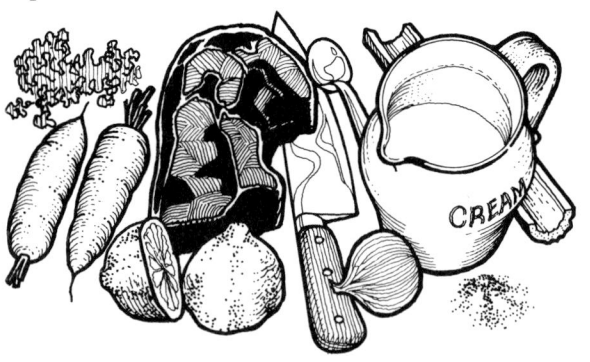

Fricassée of lamb

IMPERIAL	AMERICAN
1 lb. fillet of lamb	1 lb. lamb shoulder
1 small onion	1 small onion
2 small carrots	2 small carrots
1 stick celery	1 stalk celery
¼ teaspoon powdered mace	¼ teaspoon powdered mace
¾ pint chicken stock	scant 2 cups chicken stock
1 oz. butter	2 tablespoons butter
1 oz. flour	¼ cup all-purpose flour
1 tablespoon lemon juice	1 tablespoon lemon juice
¼ pint single cream	⅔ cup coffee cream
chopped parsley	chopped parsley

Cut the meat into small cubes, peel and slice the onion and carrots, slice the celery and place meat and vegetables in a saucepan together with the mace and stock. Bring to the boil and simmer for 1 hour, or until the lamb is tender. Strain off the stock and measure ½ pint (U.S. 1¼ cups) to use for the sauce. Place the stock in a saucepan together with the butter and flour and whisk well until the sauce thickens. Add the lemon juice and cream and return the sauce to the meat. Heat through without boiling. Serve immediately sprinkled with chopped parsley.

Stuffed lamb shoulder with apricot cups

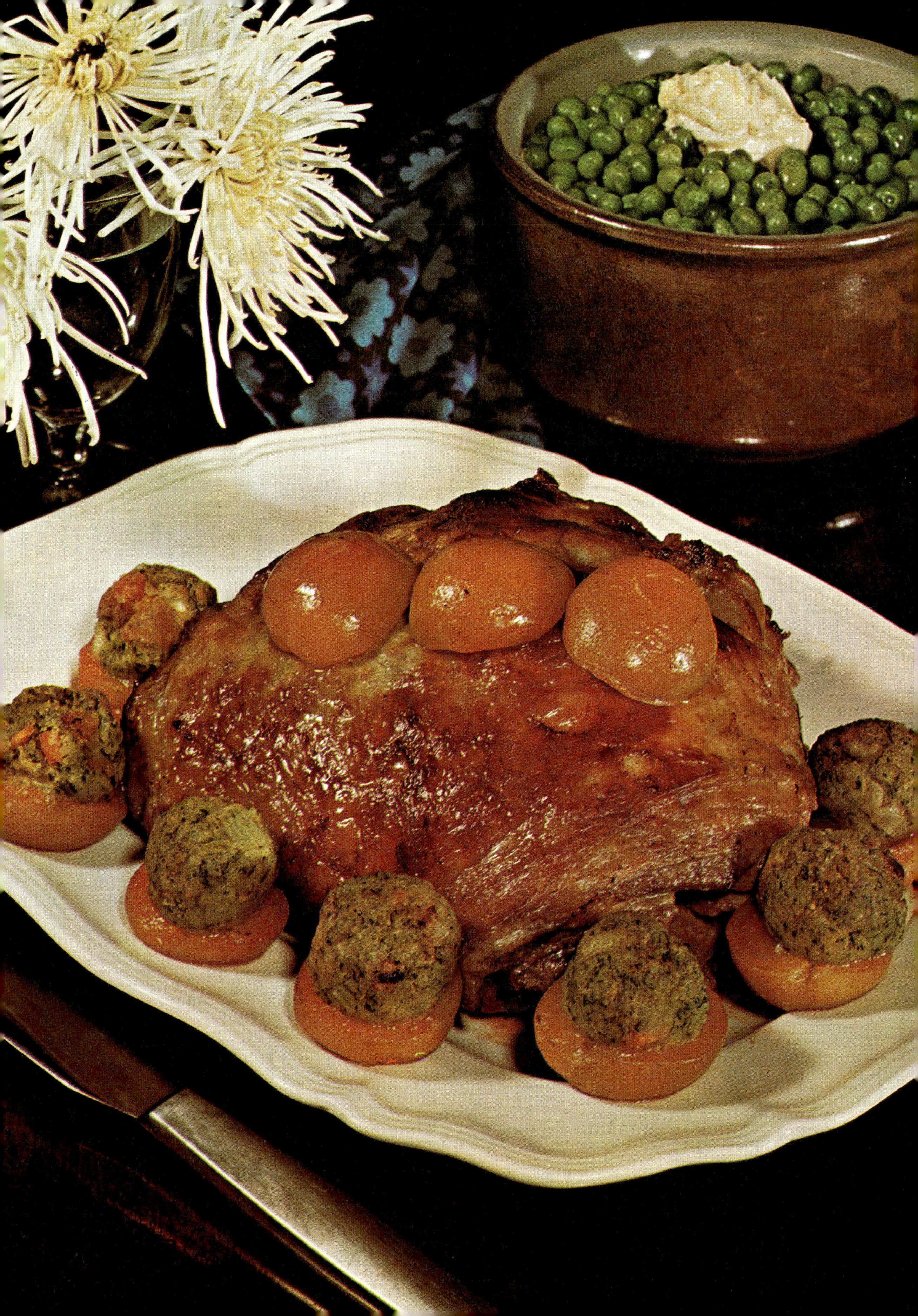

Cut the steak into small cubes. For the sauces, add mustard to one-third of the mayonnaise, tomato purée to the second third, and garlic, capers and gherkins to remainder.

Pour about two inches of oil into the fondue dish and place on the spirit burner to heat. Put the prepared sauces in small serving dishes.

Guests spear pieces of meat, place in the hot oil and leave for 1 minute or more until cooked. The meat is dipped in one of the sauces and eaten with French bread.

Fondue bourguignonne

IMPERIAL	AMERICAN
1½ lb. rump or fillet steak	1½ lb. beef fillet
oil for frying	oil for frying
½ pint mayonnaise	1¼ cups mayonnaise
1 teaspoon made mustard	1 teaspoon made mustard
1 teaspoon tomato purée	1 teaspoon tomato paste
1 clove garlic	1 clove garlic
2 teaspoons capers	2 teaspoons capers
2 small gherkins	2 sweet dill pickles
chopped parsley	chopped parsley
paprika pepper	paprika pepper

Have ready the meat cut into small, neat cubes, just large enough to spear on a long-handled fondue fork. Heat about 2 inches of oil in the fondue dish and place over a spirit burner. Guests spear pieces of meat, place in the hot oil, and leave for 1 minute or more until cooked. The cooked meat is dipped into one of the accompanying sauces and eaten with crusty French bread and red wine of the region. To make the three sauces shown here, divide the mayonnaise into three parts. To one part, add the mustard, and beat in well. Serve sprinkled with paprika pepper. To the second part, add the tomato purée and ½ teaspoon paprika pepper, beat in well, and serve sprinkled with chopped parsley. To the third part, add the crushed garlic, finely chopped capers, gherkins and 2 teaspoons chopped parsley.

Rinderrouladen*

IMPERIAL	AMERICAN
4 thin slices beef topside	4 thin slices beef round
salt and pepper to taste	salt and pepper to taste
1 tablespoon made mustard	1 tablespoon made mustard
1 onion, finely chopped	1 onion, finely chopped
4 thin rashers fat streaky bacon, de-rinded	4 bacon slices
1 large pickled cucumber	1 dill pickle
flour	flour
2 oz. butter	¼ cup butter
¼ pint beef stock	⅔ cup beef stock
1 tablespoon beurre manié, see page 7	1 tablespoon beurre manié, see page 7
2 tablespoons soured cream	3 tablespoons sour cream

Beat slices of meat between two thicknesses of greaseproof paper. Sprinkle with salt and pepper, spread with mustard and cover with onion, rashers of bacon and thin strips of pickled cucumber. Roll up from the narrow end and tie with white thread. Coat with flour. Melt the butter in a flameproof casserole and brown the rolls on all sides. Add stock and braise in a covered pan until tender. Place rolls (remove threads) on a warm serving dish, thicken the juices in the pan with beurre manié and add more seasoning if required. Stir in the soured cream and pour sauce over beef rolls.

* To freeze, pack rolls with sauce in any suitable containers. Do not add the soured cream to the sauce. Defrost, reheat and stir in the soured cream.

Boeuf en croûte

IMPERIAL	AMERICAN
Filling:	*Filling:*
½ oz. butter	1 tablespoon butter
1 small onion, chopped	1 small onion, chopped
3 dried apricots, soaked and chopped	3 dried apricots, soaked and chopped
1 oz. long-grain rice, cooked	scant ¼ cup long-grain rice, cooked
¼ teaspoon ground coriander	¼ teaspoon ground coriander
¼ teaspoon ground cumin	¼ teaspoon ground cumin
pinch chilli powder	pinch chili powder
salt and pepper to taste	salt and pepper to taste
2 lb. piece fillet of beef	2 lb. piece beef fillet
1 tablespoon corn oil	1 tablespoon corn oil
1 lb. frozen puff pastry	1 lb. frozen puff paste
beaten egg to glaze	beaten egg to glaze

To make the filling, melt the butter and fry the chopped onion until soft, add the chopped apricots, rice, spices and salt and pepper to taste. Fry for a further 5 minutes then allow to cool.

Trim the fillet, brush with corn oil and place on a baking sheet in a hot oven, 400°F, 200°C, Gas Mark 6, for 10 minutes to seal the surfaces of the meat. Cool. Roll out the pastry to an oblong shape large enough to wrap the steak in. Trim a little off the end for decoration. Place fillet in centre of pastry, cover with the filling. Fold the pastry to centre, dampen edges and seal. Turn over, seal ends and trim. Use the pastry trimmings for decoration, dampen slightly to attach. Brush with a little beaten egg to glaze and bake in a hot oven, 425°F, 220°C, Gas Mark 7, for about 30 minutes. The pastry should be golden brown and the fillet rare. Garnish with parsley sprigs and serve with a green salad or vegetables. (*Serves 6–8.*)

Note: As an alternative filling use a duxelles of mushrooms. Sauté 4 oz. mushrooms and 1 onion, finely chopped in a little butter until softened. Season with salt and pepper to taste, stir in 1 teaspoon tomato purée and if liked add 2 tablespoons red wine or 1 tablespoon brandy and continue cooking until the alcohol has evaporated.

Trim the fillet of beef; brush with corn oil and cook in a hot oven for 10 minutes to seal the surfaces of the meat. Remove from the oven and cool.

Place the partly cooked and cooled fillet on the thinly rolled pastry and cover with the rice filling. Fold the pastry to the centre, dampen edges and seal.

Bake the boeuf en croûte in a hot oven for about 30 minutes and serve garnished with parsley. The pastry should be golden brown and the fillet rare.

Pork and pear kebabs

IMPERIAL	AMERICAN
1 lb. boned belly of pork	1 lb. boneless fresh picnic shoulder
salt and pepper to taste	salt and pepper to taste
3 pears	3 pears
6 rashers streaky bacon	6 bacon slices
12 prunes	12 prunes
1 oz. butter	2 tablespoons butter
watercress sprigs to garnish	watercress sprigs to garnish

De-rind the pork and cut into neat cubes. Sprinkle with salt and pepper. Peel and core the pears and cut into small wedges. De-rind and halve the bacon rashers and wrap a piece of bacon around each piece of pear. Thread the pork, pear rolls and stoned prunes alternately on skewers and brush with melted butter. Grill for 15 minutes, turning often. Serve kebabs on a bed of fluffy boiled rice and garnish with watercress.

Ox tongue with Madeira sauce

IMPERIAL	AMERICAN
1 pickled ox tongue, approximately 4 lb.	1 pickled beef tongue, approximately 4 lb.
2 carrots	2 carrots
1 bay leaf	1 bay leaf
6 peppercorns	6 peppercorns
2 medium-sized onions	2 medium-sized onions
Sauce:	Sauce:
1 oz. butter	2 tablespoons butter
1 oz. flour	¼ cup all-purpose flour
¾ pint strained stock from the tongue	scant 2 cups strained stock from the tongue
4 tablespoons Madeira or dry sherry	⅓ cup Madeira or dry sherry
2 oz. ham, very finely chopped	¼ cup very finely chopped ham

Soak the ox tongue in cold water overnight. Curl the tongue round and either tie with string or secure with a skewer. Place in a large saucepan with the carrots, bay leaf, peppercorns and onions. Cover with water and simmer, covered, for approximately 3½ hours until the small bones at the back of the tongue can be easily removed. Take tongue from saucepan, remove bones, skin and gristle. To make the sauce melt the butter in a small saucepan, stir in the flour and cook until golden brown. Add the strained stock and the Madeira. Stir in the ham, bring to the boil and simmer gently for a few minutes to reduce slightly. Serve with the sliced tongue.

Korma kebabs

IMPERIAL	AMERICAN
1½ tablespoons curry powder	2 tablespoons curry powder
1 tablespoon corn oil	1 tablespoon corn oil
1 tablespoon wine vinegar	1 tablespoon wine vinegar
¼ pint natural yogurt	⅔ cup natural yogurt
salt and pepper to taste	salt and pepper to taste
1 lb. fillet of lamb, in 1-inch cubes	1 lb. lamb shoulder, in 1-inch cubes

Mix together the curry powder, oil, vinegar, yogurt and seasoning and use to marinate the meat, overnight if possible. Thread the meat on skewers and grill for 15 minutes, turning and basting with the marinade. Serve with boiled rice and a green salad.

Rich beef stew with mustard croûtons*

(Illustrated in colour on the opposite page)

IMPERIAL	AMERICAN
1½ lb. stewing steak	1½ lb. beef stew meat
1 tablespoon corn oil	1 tablespoon corn oil
1 large onion	1 large onion
salt and pepper to taste	salt and pepper to taste
1 tablespoon French mustard	1 tablespoon French mustard
1 beef stock cube	1 beef bouillon cube
2 oz. raisins	⅓ cup raisins
¾ pint light ale	scant 2 cups light beer
½ oz. cornflour	2 tablespoons cornstarch
Mustard croûtons:	Mustard croûtons:
2 slices stale white bread	2 slices stale white bread
1 teaspoon dry mustard	1 teaspoon dry mustard
oil for frying	oil for frying
chopped parsley to garnish	chopped parsley to garnish

Cut the meat into even-sized dice. Heat the corn oil in a flameproof casserole and sauté the peeled and chopped onion and meat in it until brown. Add salt and pepper to taste, French mustard, stock cube and raisins. Stir in the ale, bring to the boil, cover and simmer gently until the meat is tender, about 1½ hours. Moisten the cornflour with a little cold water, stir into the casserole, bring to the boil stirring all the time. Cook a further 3 minutes. To make the croûtons, cut bread into small triangles. Place in a shallow bowl and sift mustard over them through a sieve, shaking the bowl gently to coat the bread. Fry in very hot oil until golden brown on both sides. Drain well. Garnish stew with croûtons. Sprinkle each croûton with chopped parsley.

* To freeze, pack stew and croûtons separately. Garnish with parsley when serving.

Rich beef stew with mustard croûtons

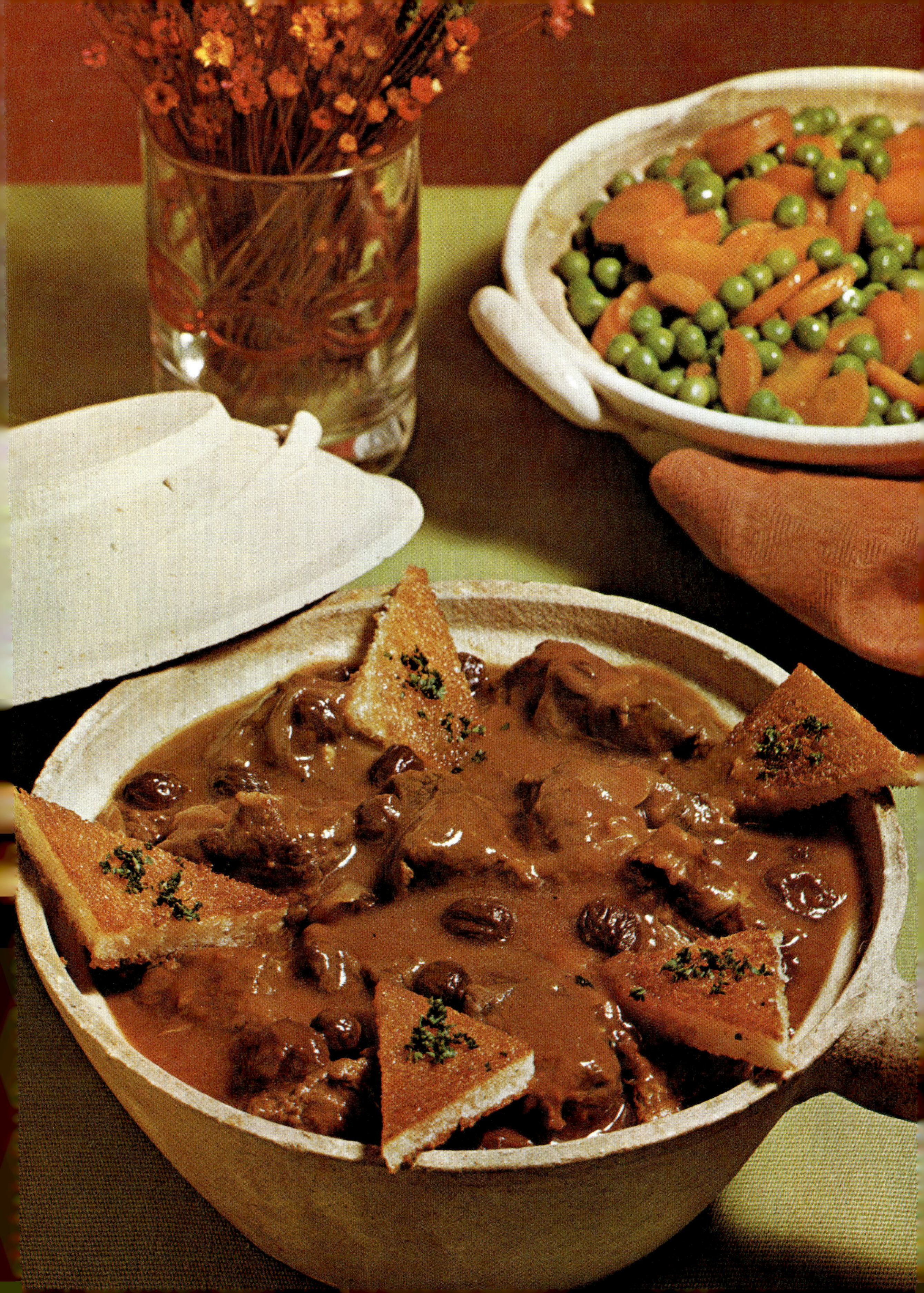

Trim the outer skin from the pork chops and make a slit along the fat side of the chops to form a pocket inside the meat.

Fill the pocket in each chop with some of the prepared stuffing, then brown the chops on both sides in the oil in the ovenproof casserole.

Serve the chops from the ovenproof casserole and garnish with a sprig of parsley. If liked serve with floury boiled or baked potatoes.

Pocket-stuffed pork chops

IMPERIAL	AMERICAN
4 thick pork chops	4 thick pork chops
1 small onion	1 small onion
1 small green pepper	1 small green sweet pepper
1 medium-sized cooking apple	1 medium-sized baking apple
4 stuffed green olives	4 stuffed green olives
salt and freshly ground black pepper to taste	salt and freshly ground black pepper to taste
1 oz. butter	2 tablespoons butter
2 tablespoons corn oil	3 tablespoons corn oil

Trim the outer skin from the pork chops. Make a slit along the fat side of the chops, to form a pocket inside the meat. Peel and finely chop the onion, deseed and finely chop the green pepper; peel, core and chop the apple and thinly slice the stuffed olives. Mix these ingredients together with the seasonings and sauté this mixture lightly for 3–4 minutes in the butter. Fill each pocket with the stuffing, brown the chops on both sides in the oil in an ovenproof casserole. Cover and bake in a moderate oven, 350°F, 180°C, Gas Mark 4, for 40–45 minutes, basting from time to time. Garnish with parsley and serve with floury boiled or baked potatoes.

Cutlets à la milanaise*

IMPERIAL	AMERICAN
1 lb. lamb cutlets	1 lb. lamb loin chops
4 oz. butter, melted	½ cup butter, melted
2 oz. Cheddar cheese, finely grated	½ cup finely grated Cheddar cheese
2 oz. Parmesan cheese, finely grated	½ cup finely grated Parmesan cheese
4 oz. fine fresh white breadcrumbs	2 cups fresh soft bread crumbs
1 egg, lightly beaten	1 egg, lightly beaten
2 oz. butter	¼ cup butter
1 tablespoon oil	1 tablespoon oil

Wipe and trim the cutlets, dip in melted butter then in the mixture of grated cheese and breadcrumbs, pressing on well. Dip carefully in the beaten egg and again in the cheese and breadcrumb mixture. Melt the butter and oil in a heavy frying pan and seal the outside of the cutlets over high heat. Reduce heat to cook slowly for 10 minutes each side and avoid overbrowning the coating. Turn very carefully without piercing the coating. Serve with pasta spirals or shells and tomato sauce (see page 74).

* To freeze, pack cooked in a plastic container with foil dividers between the cutlets. To reheat and serve put on a baking sheet and place in a moderately hot oven for 30 minutes.

Pressed ox tongue

IMPERIAL	AMERICAN
1 ox tongue, cooked as described on page 58	1 beef tongue, cooked as described on page 58
2 teaspoons gelatine	2 teaspoons gelatin
¼ pint strained stock from the tongue	⅔ cup strained stock from the tongue

Place the tongue tightly curled in a round dish. Moisten the gelatine with a little cold water and add the remaining stock which must be hot. Stir until the gelatine has dissolved then pour over the tongue. If you prefer the jelly can be lightly coloured with gravy browning. Place a small plate over the tongue, top with a weight and allow to set. To turn out, hold the base of the dish in hot water for a few seconds and then invert on to a serving plate. Serve garnished with assorted salad vegetables.

Stuffed loin of veal with pineapple

IMPERIAL	AMERICAN
1 15-oz. can pineapple rings	1 15-oz. can pineapple rings
4 oz. fat streaky bacon, de-rinded and chopped	¼ lb. bacon slices, chopped
1 packet parsley and thyme stuffing	1 package parsley and thyme stuffing
zest and juice 1 lemon	zest and juice 1 lemon
1 loin of veal, about 3–4 lb.	1 veal loin roast, about 3–4 lb.
2 oz. butter	¼ cup butter
2 tablespoons corn oil	3 tablespoons corn oil
glacé cherries	candied cherries
1 1-lb. 3-oz. can new potatoes	1 1-lb. 3-oz. can new potatoes

Drain syrup from pineapple, reserve three rings for garnish and chop the rest finely. Fry bacon gently to extract the fat and turn contents of frying pan into a basin with the packet stuffing, lemon zest and juice, chopped pineapple and syrup. Add sufficient boiling water to make a firm stuffing. Bone the meat and use bone to make a stock for the gravy while joint is roasting. Pack stuffing into the cavity and sew with trussing needle and fine string, or skewer together. Allow room for stuffing to swell. Place in a greased roasting pan. Melt butter and oil together, pour over joint, cover with foil and roast in a moderate oven, 350°F, 180°C, Gas Mark 4, for about 2 hours (see chart on page 9). Place the cooked joint on a warm serving dish, garnish with remaining pineapple and glacé cherries, secured with wooden cocktail sticks. Heat the potatoes, drain and use to surround the joint. Serve the gravy separately.

Bone the loin of veal and use the bone to make a stock for the gravy while the joint is roasting. Prepare the parsley and thyme stuffing.

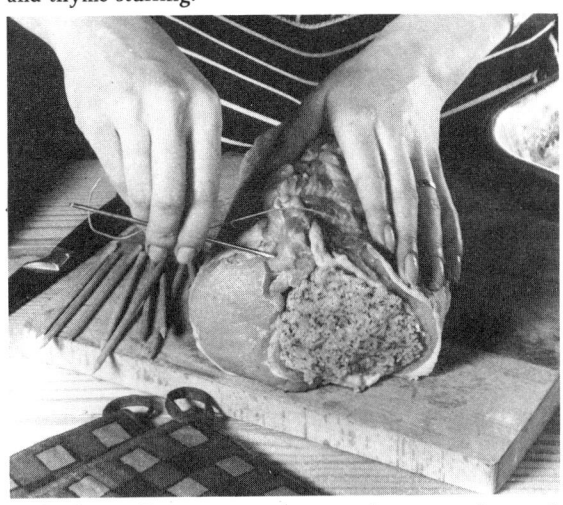

Pack the stuffing into the cavity and sew together with a trussing needle and fine string, allow room for the stuffing to swell.

Place the cooked loin on a warm serving dish and serve garnished with the canned pineapple rings and glacé cherries and surrounded with new potatoes.

Creamed sweetbreads with mushrooms

IMPERIAL	AMERICAN
1 lb. lamb's sweetbreads	1 lb. lamb sweetbreads
1 oz. butter	2 tablespoons butter
4 oz. mushrooms	$\frac{1}{4}$ lb. mushrooms
1 oz. flour	$\frac{1}{4}$ cup all-purpose flour
$\frac{1}{4}$ pint milk	$\frac{2}{3}$ cup milk
1 chicken stock cube	1 chicken bouillon cube
salt and pepper to taste	salt and pepper to taste
4 tablespoons single cream	$\frac{1}{3}$ cup coffee cream
fleurons, see page 76	fleurons, see page 76

To blanch the sweetbreads, place in cold water, bring slowly to the boil and remove from heat. Drain sweetbreads, reserving the liquid. Trim and chop roughly. Melt the butter, sauté the mushrooms and sweetbreads lightly in it, stir in the flour and cook for $\frac{1}{2}$ minute. Add the milk and the chicken stock cube dissolved in $\frac{1}{4}$ pint (U.S. $\frac{2}{3}$ cup) of the blanching liquid. Season to taste, bring to the boil, stirring, and simmer for about 15 minutes, or until the sweetbreads are tender. Stir in the cream, reheat and serve at once with fleurons, or use as a filling for large vol-au-vent cases.

Roast pork with carnival apples

(Illustrated in colour on the back cover)

IMPERIAL	AMERICAN
1 small leg of pork	1 small fresh ham
salt for sprinkling	salt for sprinkling
1 packet parsley and thyme stuffing	1 package parsley and thyme stuffing
6 red-skinned dessert apples	6 red-skinned dessert apples
flour	flour

Have the skin of the pork well scored, sprinkle with salt and roast according to the chart on page 9. One hour before the joint is cooked, make up the packet of stuffing. Core the apples, score with a *cannel* knife or sharp pointed potato peeler to give a striped effect. Fill the centres of the apples with half the stuffing mixture and form the remainder into small balls with floured hands. Place on top of the apples. Spoon surplus fat from roasting pan. Bake stuffed apples round the joint, brushing well with the fat, and again towards the end of cooking time. Serve the joint surrounded with the stuffed apples, and use the pan juices to make a thick gravy. (If the roasting pan is not large enough, cook apples, well brushed with pork fat, in separate pan.) Serve with celery hearts.

Rognons sautés au vin rouge

(Illustrated in colour on the opposite page)

IMPERIAL	AMERICAN
12 lamb's kidneys	12 lamb kidneys
4 oz. streaky bacon	$\frac{1}{4}$ lb. bacon slices
1 oz. butter	2 tablespoons butter
1 small onion	1 small onion
salt and pepper to taste	salt and pepper to taste
4 oz. button mushrooms	$\frac{1}{4}$ lb. button mushrooms
2 teaspoons flour	2 teaspoons all-purpose flour
$\frac{1}{4}$ pint dry red wine	$\frac{2}{3}$ cup dry red wine
1 beef stock cube	1 beef bouillon cube
2 tablespoons chopped parsley	3 tablespoons chopped parsley

Slice kidneys, removing fibres and fat. De-rind and chop half the bacon and form the rest into small rolls. Melt the butter in a casserole. Peel and chop the onion and sauté in the butter with the chopped bacon, stirring for a few minutes. Season to taste with salt and pepper. Add the kidneys and sliced mushrooms and continue to cook for a further 3 minutes. Add the flour, stir well to blend, add the wine and stock cube dissolved in $\frac{1}{2}$ pint (U.S. $1\frac{1}{4}$ cups) boiling water. Reduce heat and cover, simmer until kidneys are tender. Meanwhile fry bacon rolls. Serve kidneys in a hot dish garnished with the bacon rolls and sprinkled with parsley.

Brains with black butter

IMPERIAL	AMERICAN
1 lb. calf's brains	1 lb. calf brains
$\frac{3}{4}$ pint chicken stock	scant 2 cups chicken stock
4 oz. butter	$\frac{1}{2}$ cup butter
juice 1 lemon	juice 1 lemon
1 tablespoon chopped parsley	1 tablespoon chopped parsley

Soak the brains in cold water to remove traces of blood. Drain well, bring to the boil in the chicken stock and simmer gently for 20 minutes. Remove, drain well and cut into $\frac{1}{2}$-inch slices. Heat the butter until it begins to turn golden brown, add the brains and cook gently for 5 minutes. Stir in the lemon juice and serve at once, sprinkled with parsley.

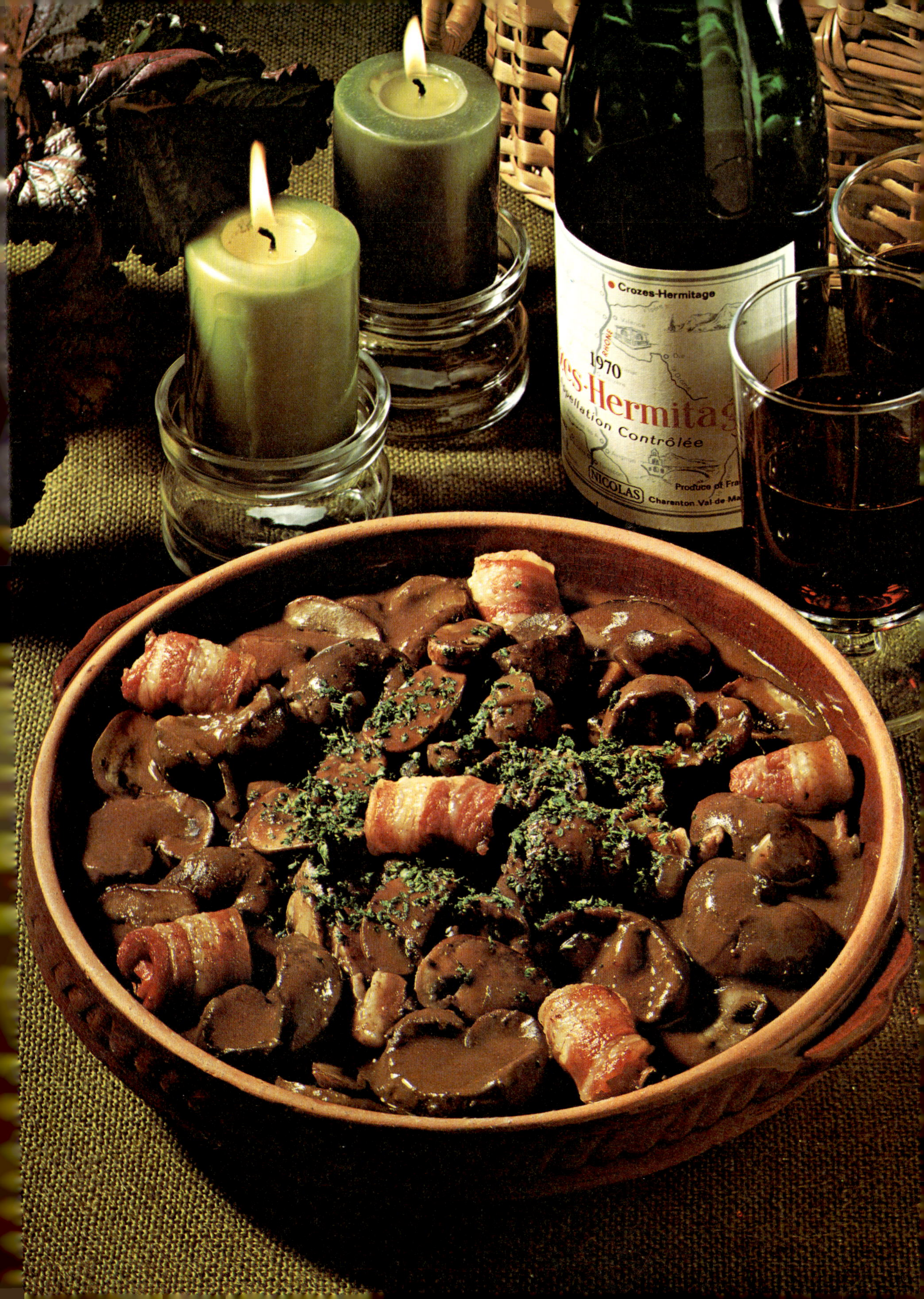
Crozes-Hermitage
1970
Contrôlée
NICOLAS

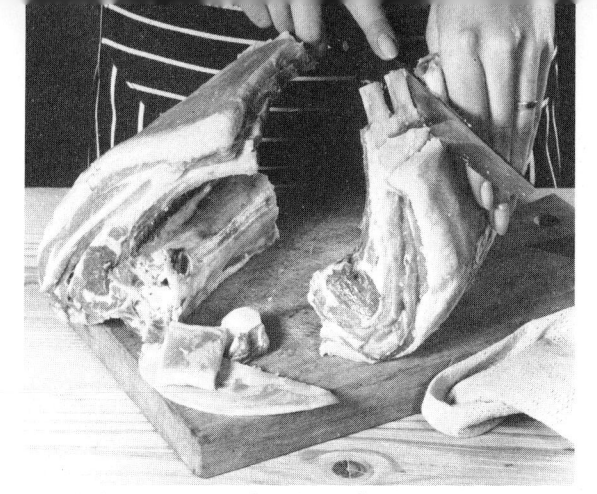

Cut the fat away across the whole of each best end of neck. Trim down between each cutlet bone so that the bones are left bare.

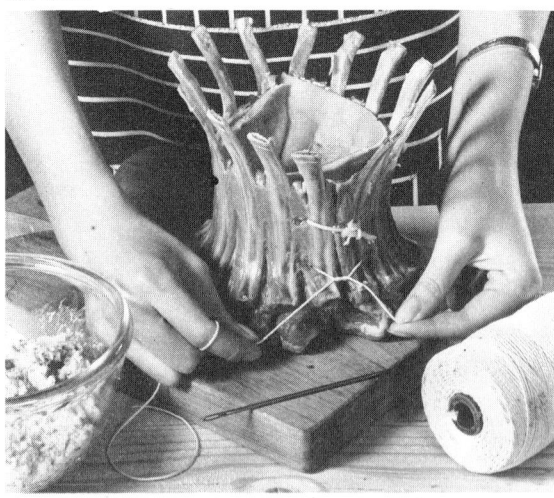

Form the two best ends of neck into a semi-circle, skin side outwards, and secure with string near the base and just below where the bones have been cleaned.

Place the cooked cauliflower in the centre of the crown and top alternate bones with cutlet frills. Garnish with parsley and serve with roast potatoes.

Crown roast of lamb

IMPERIAL	AMERICAN
2 best ends of neck of lamb, 6 bones each	2 racks of lamb, 6 bones each
few cutlet frills	few paper frills
1 small whole cooked cauliflower	1 small whole cooked cauliflower

To prepare the crown Cut the fat away 3 inches in towards the end of the meat across the whole best end of neck. Then trim down between the cutlet bones with a small knife, removing all meat and fat, so that the ends of the bones are left bare. Strip off the skin. Treat the other best end in the same way. With the point of the knife, make a slit between each cutlet and the next at the base, so that you can bring the two pieces of meat round, skin side outwards, each in a semi-circle, to meet and form a full circle. You must have pieces with at least six bones each to enable you to make the circle. Sew the ends together, near the base at one side using a trussing needle and fine string and just below the point to which the bones have been cleaned. Sew the other open ends together. You can use wooden skewers, which most butchers supply, instead, to form the meat securely into a circle.

To cook the crown Place in a roasting pan, well greased to prevent the joint from sticking. Cover the tips of the bones with foil or greaseproof paper to prevent them from burning, and place in a moderately hot oven, 375°F, 190°C, Gas Mark 5, for 1 hour. Place the cooked cauliflower in the centre of the crown, top the alternate bones with cutlet frills; garnish with parsley and serve with roast potatoes.

Note: The crown may be filled with a stuffing mixture before roasting. Use any well seasoned stuffing suitable for lamb and remember to allow additional cooking time.

New Zealand guard of honour

(Illustrated in colour on the front cover and page 27)

This is also a very professional looking roast, even easier to cook and serve. The two best ends of lamb must each have the same number of cutlets, five, six or seven. Remove the chine bone from each joint, trim and clean bone tips of 1½ inches of fat. Place the two joints together in a roasting pan, pressing the bones together to cross in the centre and protrude at each side. Pad the bone tips and roast as for crown roast of lamb. To serve, top bone tips with cutlet frills and glacé cherries; garnish with parsley and serve with roast potatoes.

Blender pâtés

Potted beef

IMPERIAL	AMERICAN
1 lb. stewing steak	1 lb. beef stew meat
¼ pint stock	⅔ cup stock
½ onion	½ onion
1 bay leaf	1 bay leaf
salt and pepper to taste	salt and pepper to taste
1 oz. butter	2 tablespoons butter
1 clove garlic (optional)	1 clove garlic (optional)

Cut the meat into cubes and place in a casserole with the stock, onion, bay leaf and seasonings. Cover and cook in a moderate oven, 350°F, 180°C, Gas Mark 4, for about 2 hours, or until the meat is tender. Strain off the stock and reserve. Remove bay leaf and onion. Add the butter and about 4 tablespoons (U.S. ⅓ cup) of the stock to the meat then put half this mixture in the blender goblet and liquidise until smooth. Repeat with the remaining mixture and add the crushed garlic at this stage if used. The mixture can be used at once, or spooned into individual dishes and covered with clarified butter (see page 7).

Yeoman's pâté

IMPERIAL	AMERICAN
1 bay leaf	1 bay leaf
12 rashers streaky bacon	12 bacon slices
8 oz. pig's liver	½ lb. pork liver
1 clove garlic	1 clove garlic
6 anchovy fillets	6 anchovy fillets
2 tablespoons sherry	3 tablespoons sherry
1 teaspoon salt	1 teaspoon salt
pinch pepper	pinch pepper
½ pint béchamel sauce	1¼ cups béchamel sauce

Prepare a 1-lb. loaf tin by placing the bay leaf in the bottom, de-rinding and stretching eight of the bacon rashers with a knife and pressing round the sides and base of the tin. De-rind the remaining bacon rashers and cut into pieces, fry these gently until the fat begins to run. Cut the liver into pieces and fry in the bacon fat for a few minutes. Add the fried bacon and liver, together with the garlic, anchovies, sherry, salt and pepper, to the sauce and stir well. Pour half this mixture into the blender goblet and liquidise until smooth. Repeat with the other half and place the pâté mixture in the loaf tin. Cover with foil, place the tin in a bain-marie and cook in a moderate oven, 350°F, 180°C, Gas Mark 4, for 1–1½ hours until the juice from the pâté is no longer pink. Serve cold.

Cut the stewing steak into cubes and cook it in the oven with the stock, onion, bay leaf and seasonings for about 2 hours. Strain and reserve stock.

Add the butter and about 4 tablespoons of the stock to the meat and put this mixture (and crushed garlic, if used) half at a time, in the blender goblet.

The mixture can be used at once, or spooned into individual dishes and for longer storage covered with clarified butter. Serve from the dishes.

Lone cook

Tasty pork mince

IMPERIAL	AMERICAN
½ oz. butter	1 tablespoon butter
1 small onion, chopped	1 small onion, chopped
8 oz. minced blade bone of pork or beef	½ lb. ground pork or beef
1 8-oz. can tomatoes	1 8-oz. can tomatoes
2 oz. mushrooms, sliced	¼ cup sliced mushrooms
½ teaspoon dried sage	½ teaspoon dried sage
salt and pepper to taste	salt and pepper to taste

Melt the butter and fry onion and pork gently for 10 minutes. Add the tomatoes, mushrooms, sage and seasoning and heat through. Transfer mixture to an ovenproof dish and cook in a moderate oven, 350°F, 180°C, Gas Mark 4 for 1 hour. Left-over mince can be used in the following recipe.

Cheesy-stuffed tomatoes

IMPERIAL	AMERICAN
2 large tomatoes	2 large tomatoes
2 teaspoons grated onion	2 teaspoon grated onion
1 tablespoon grated Cheddar cheese	1 tablespoon grated Cheddar cheese
1 tablespoon fresh white breadcrumbs	1 tablespoon fresh soft bread crumbs
2 oz. cooked minced beef or pork	about ½ cup cooked ground beef or pork
salt and pepper to taste	salt and pepper to taste

Remove the top from each tomato and scoop out the centre. Combine the onion, cheese, breadcrumbs, meat and seasonings and use to stuff the tomatoes. Place tomatoes in a greased ovenproof dish, surround with the tomato pulp and 2 tablespoons (U.S. 3 tablespoons) water and bake in a moderately hot oven, 400°F, 200°C, Gas Mark 6, for 20 minutes.

Beef olives in mushroom sauce

IMPERIAL	AMERICAN
½ packet onion and mushroom stuffing	½ package onion and mushroom stuffing
2 thin slices topside of beef	2 thin slices beef round
1 6-oz. can condensed mushroom soup	1 6-oz. can condensed mushroom soup

Make up the stuffing according to the directions on the packet. Divide stuffing between the two slices of beef and roll up firmly. Put the rolls into an ovenproof casserole and pour over the slightly diluted soup. Bake in the centre of a moderately hot oven, 375°F, 190°C, Gas Mark 5, for 45 minutes.

Grilled sausages and pineapple

IMPERIAL	AMERICAN
½ oz. butter	1 tablespoon butter
4 spring onions, trimmed and chopped	4 scallions, trimmed and chopped
1 8-oz. can pineapple pieces, drained	1 8-oz. can pineapple pieces, drained
1 8-oz. can baked beans	1 8-oz. can baked beans
salt and pepper to taste	salt and pepper to taste
4 pork chipolata sausages	4 all-pork sausages

Melt the butter and lightly sauté the onions and well drained pineapple pieces for 1 minute. Stir in the baked beans and 2 tablespoons (U.S. 3 tablespoons) pineapple syrup. Season to taste. Meanwhile grill or fry the sausages and serve on top of the bean and pineapple mixture.

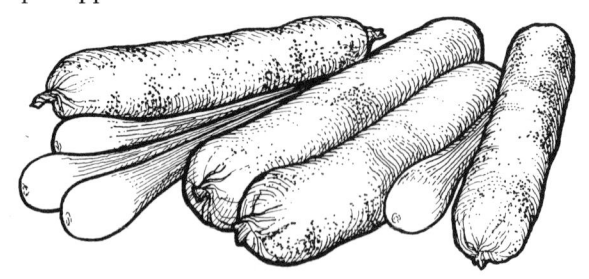

Wineseller's beefsteak

IMPERIAL	AMERICAN
1 oz. butter	2 tablespoons butter
1 teaspoon oil	1 teaspoon oil
1 entrecôte or rump steak	1 rib or club steak
salt and freshly ground pepper to taste	salt and freshly ground pepper to taste
2 tablespoons red wine	3 tablespoons red wine

Heat half the butter and the oil in a small frying pan and fry the steak for 4–5 minutes on each side, according to whether desired medium, rare or well done. Remove steak, sprinkle with salt and pepper and keep hot. Add the wine to the pan and boil fast, stirring with a spoon, until the liquid is reduced to about 2 tablespoons (U.S. 3 tablespoons). Remove from the heat and stir in the remaining butter. Pour over the steak and serve.

Twosome specials

Bobotee

IMPERIAL	AMERICAN
small knob butter	small knob butter
1 teaspoon oil	1 teaspoon oil
1 onion, sliced	1 onion, sliced
12 oz. minced beef	¾ lb. ground beef
pinch garlic powder	pinch garlic powder
2 teaspoons curry powder	2 teaspoons curry powder
2 teaspoons mango chutney	2 teaspoon mango chutney
1 tablespoon chopped almonds	1 tablespoon chopped almonds
salt and pepper to taste	salt and pepper to taste
½ slice white bread	½ slice white bread
little milk	little milk
1 egg, lightly beaten	1 egg, lightly beaten

Heat the butter and oil in a frying pan and sauté the onion until softened. Add the meat and cook gently until it changes colour. Add the garlic powder, curry powder, chutney, almonds and seasoning. Trim crusts from the bread and soak in a little milk, add to the meat and mix in well. Add a little water or stock to almost cover the meat, bring to the boil and simmer for 30–40 minutes, until the meat is cooked and most of the liquid has evaporated. Add half the beaten egg to the meat mixture, stir well and pour into an ovenproof dish. Pour the remaining egg over the meat and cook in a moderate oven, 350°F, 180°C, Gas Mark 4 for 20 minutes, until the egg is well set. Serve with fluffy boiled rice.

Beef-stuffed peppers

IMPERIAL	AMERICAN
4 green peppers	4 green sweet peppers
1 tablespoon sage and onion stuffing mix	1 tablespoon sage and onion stuffing mix
1½ oz. butter, melted	3 tablespoons butter, melted
8 oz. cooked beef, minced	1½ cups cooked ground beef
1 large pickled cucumber, finely chopped	1 dill pickle, finely chopped
salt and pepper to taste	salt and pepper to taste

Slice tops off the peppers and take out core and seeds. Bind together stuffing mix, butter, minced beef, cucumber and seasoning. Moisten with boiling water and use to fill the peppers. Replace lids, arrange in an ovenproof casserole, cover and bake in a moderately hot oven, 400°F, 200°C, Gas Mark 6, for 35–45 minutes, until the peppers are tender and filling cooked.

Note: This recipe makes good use of the remains of a small joint.

Lamb pilau

IMPERIAL	AMERICAN
12 oz. boned stewing lamb	¾ lb. boneless lamb stew meat
½ oz. seasoned flour	2 tablespoons seasoned flour
2 tablespoons oil	3 tablespoons oil
1 small pepper	1 small sweet pepper
1 large onion	1 large onion
2 tomatoes	2 tomatoes
½ oz. raisins	about 2 tablespoons raisins
1 tablespoon lemon juice	1 tablespoon lemon juice
4 oz. long-grain rice	generous ½ cup long-grain rice
½ pint chicken stock	1¼ cups chicken stock

Dice the lamb, toss in the seasoned flour and sauté in the heated oil to brown on all sides. Remove and keep hot. Core and slice the pepper and peel and slice the onion. Sauté these in the remaining oil, add the chopped tomatoes, raisins, lemon juice, rice and boiling stock. Place in an ovenproof casserole, add the lamb and cook in a moderate oven, 350°F, 180°C, Gas Mark 4, for 30–35 minutes until the rice has absorbed all the liquid. Serve immediately.

Note: This quantity will provide two meals, as any leftover can be reheated with extra liquid.

Steak-stuffed courgettes

IMPERIAL	AMERICAN
1 tablespoon oil	1 tablespoon oil
1 small onion, chopped	1 small onion, chopped
4 oz. rump steak, chopped	¼ lb. steak, chopped
1 tablespoon tomato purée	1 tablespoon tomato paste
½ teaspoon French mustard	½ teaspoon French mustard
¼ pint stock	⅔ cup stock
½ teaspoon vinegar	½ teaspoon vinegar
salt and pepper to taste	salt and pepper to taste
4 small courgettes	4 small zucchini

Heat the oil and fry onion gently until golden. Add meat, raise heat and stir until it changes colour. Add tomato purée, mustard, 1 tablespoon stock, vinegar and seasoning. Cut a deep V-shaped wedge from the length of each courgette and fill with the steak mixture. Place in an ovenproof dish, pour rest of stock round them, cover with foil and cook in a moderate oven, 350°F, 180°C, Gas Mark 4, for 45 minutes–1 hour, until the courgettes are cooked. Bake 2 small potatoes wrapped in foil, at the same time.

Roll out the pastry thinly and cut into four 1-inch circles. Place a little of the filling in the centre of each circle. Add seasoning to taste.

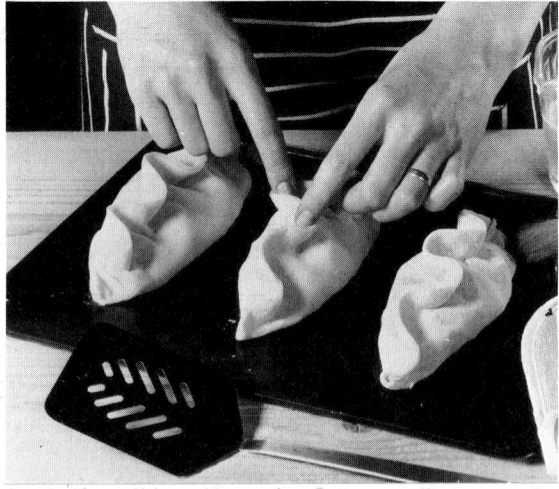

Brush the edges with water; bring together over the filling, seal and flute. Brush with milk and bake in a moderately hot oven.

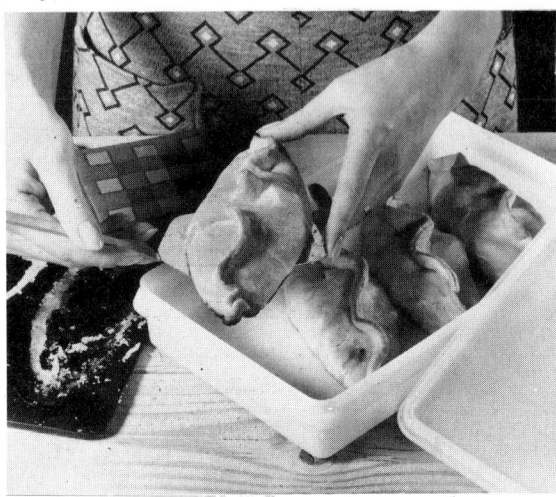

When cooked and completely cold place pasties in a rigid-based plastic container for freezing. To defrost and reheat place in a hot oven for 30 minutes.

Cumberland kidneys

IMPERIAL	AMERICAN
½ oz. butter	1 tablespoon butter
1 small onion, thinly sliced	1 small onion, thinly sliced
4 lamb's kidneys	4 lamb kidneys
2 oz. mushrooms, quartered	½ cup quartered mushrooms
1 tablespoon brown table sauce	dash each Worcestershire and Tabasco sauce
1 teaspoon cornflour	1 teaspoon cornstarch
2 teaspoons water	2 teaspoons water
2 teaspoons redcurrant jelly	2 teaspoons redcurrant jelly
2 teaspoons grated orange zest	2 teaspoons grated orange zest
salt and pepper to taste	salt and pepper to taste

Heat the butter in a pan and fry the onion gently for 5 minutes. Cut the kidneys in half, skin and remove cores. Add kidneys and mushrooms to the pan and fry for a further 5 minutes, stirring occasionally. Stir in the sauce. Blend cornflour with water, stir into the pan and bring to the boil. Add the redcurrant jelly, orange zest and seasoning and cook gently for a further 5 minutes. Serve on a bed of fluffy boiled rice.

Cornish pasties*

IMPERIAL	AMERICAN
12 oz. short crust pastry	basic pie dough using 3 cups all-purpose flour etc.
Filling:	*Filling:*
1 onion, chopped	1 onion, chopped
1 potato, diced	1 potato, diced
1 swede, diced	1 swede, diced
8 oz. good stewing steak, diced	½ lb. good beef stew meat, diced
salt and pepper to taste	salt and pepper to taste
milk to glaze	milk to glaze

Roll out the pastry thinly and cut four 7-inch circles. Divide the filling between the circles, season and brush the edges with water. Bring edges together over the filling and seal well. Flute the edges and place pasties on a greased baking sheet, brush with milk and bake in a moderately hot oven, 400°F, 200°C, Gas Mark 6, for the first 30 minutes then reduce to very moderate, 325°F, 170°C, Gas Mark 3, for a further 35–40 minutes until filling is cooked and the pasties are golden brown.

* To freeze, when completely cold, place in a rigid-based plastic container and seal. To defrost and reheat, place in a hot oven, 425°F, 220°C, Gas Mark 7, for 30 minutes.

Invalid dishes

Beef tea

IMPERIAL	AMERICAN
1 lb. flank or skirt of beef	1 lb. beef flank or plate
1 pint water	2½ cups water
½ teaspoon salt	½ teaspoon salt

Remove all fat from the meat. Place meat in a basin with the water and salt and place the basin over a saucepan of boiling water. Cover and simmer for 2–3 hours then strain carefully. Allow to cool, skim off fat and when required reheat without boiling and serve with biscuits or toast.

Variation:

Beef tea custard

IMPERIAL	AMERICAN
¼ pint beef tea	⅔ cup beef tea
1 egg	1 egg
1 egg yolk	1 egg yolk
salt to taste	salt to taste

Place the beef tea in a basin, beat in the egg and egg yolk and season to taste. Pour the mixture into a well-greased cup. Cover with foil or greaseproof and place in a saucepan containing sufficient boiling water to come half way up the cup. Steam very gently for 20 minutes and then turn out carefully on to a plate. Serve on its own, hot or cold, or diced in broth or soup.

Meat and potato soufflé

IMPERIAL	AMERICAN
3 oz. smooth mashed potato	scant ½ cup smooth mashed potato
1–2 tablespoons milk or cream	2–3 tablespoons milk or cream
3 oz. minced cooked beef, lamb or veal	scant ¾ cup ground cooked beef, lamb or veal
salt and pepper to taste	salt and pepper to taste
1 large egg, separated	1 egg, separated

Place potatoes in a basin and mix in sufficient milk or cream to obtain a soft consistency. Add meat and seasoning and mix well. Beat egg yolk into mixture. Whip the egg white stiffly and fold in. Place mixture in a well-greased individual soufflé dish. Bake in a moderately hot oven, 375°F, 190°C, Gas Mark 5, for about 20 minutes, until golden brown.

Raw beef sandwiches

IMPERIAL	AMERICAN
2–3 oz. lean juicy steak	2–3 oz. beef fillet
salt and pepper to taste	salt and pepper to taste
thin slices buttered bread	thin slices buttered bread

Scrape the meat and season lightly. If necessary rub through a sieve, to eliminate every piece of stringy sinew. Make into sandwiches with the buttered bread and cut into dainty pieces.

Braised liver and bacon

IMPERIAL	AMERICAN
4 oz. ox liver, sliced	¼ lb. beef liver, sliced
little milk	little milk
1 tablespoon seasoned flour	1 tablespoon seasoned flour
1 tablespoon oil	1 tablespoon oil
2 oz. streaky bacon, diced	⅓ cup diced bacon slices
1 small onion, sliced	1 small onion, sliced
1 small carrot, sliced	1 small carrot, sliced
¼ pint beef stock	⅔ cup beef stock
salt and pepper to taste	salt and pepper to taste

Cover liver with milk, allow to stand at least 1 hour, drain, pat dry and coat in some of the seasoned flour. Heat the oil and sauté the liver on both sides in a flameproof casserole to brown. Add the bacon, onion and carrot, brown slightly then stir in the remaining flour. Pour in the stock and season to taste. Cover and simmer for 1 hour. Serve with creamy mashed potatoes.

Calf's foot broth

IMPERIAL	AMERICAN
1 calf's foot	1 calf foot
3 pints water	7½ cups water
grated zest 1 lemon	grated zest 1 lemon
salt and pepper to taste	salt and pepper to taste
1 egg yolk	1 egg yolk
2 tablespoons milk	3 tablespoons milk

Wash the calf's foot, simmer in the water for 3 hours and then strain into a basin. When cold, skim off fat and reheat the broth with the lemon rind, removing this when sufficient flavour has been imparted. Season to taste. To ½ pint (U.S. 1¼ cups) of the broth, add the egg yolk and the milk. Stir over low heat until thickened but do not boil. Serve hot. The remaining broth can be reduced by half, strained and allowed to set into jelly.

Marinades and stuffings

Marinades To marinate meat means to soak it in a mixture of oil, wine or vinegar and herbs and spices for several hours. As well as adding flavour, this helps to moisturise a dry meat and to tenderise tough, cheaper cuts of meat. The meat can also be cooked in or basted with the marinade. For joints of meat a polythene bag is best for enclosing the meat with the marinade. Tie the top loosely. To marinate diced meat or small cuts, place in a shallow china dish and cover. Here is a typical recipe for a marinade.

Traditional marinade

IMPERIAL	AMERICAN
1 carrot	1 carrot
1 onion or 2 shallots	1 onion or 2 shallots
2 cloves garlic	2 cloves garlic
½ pint red wine	1¼ cups red wine
4 tablespoons wine vinegar	⅓ cup wine vinegar
1 tablespoon corn oil	1 tablespoon corn oil
3 bay leaves	3 bay leaves
3 parsley stalks	3 parsley stalks
sprigs of thyme, rosemary and juniper berries if available	sprigs of thyme, rosemary and juniper berries if available
1½ teaspoons salt	1½ teaspoons salt
6 peppercorns	6 peppercorns

Peel and slice the carrot and onion and crush the garlic. Place all the ingredients in a saucepan and bring to the boil. Remove from heat and cool before using with joints of pork or beef. Marinate the meat in a polythene bag, loosely tied, in the refrigerator overnight. Then use the marinade, strained, for basting during roasting.

Cider marinade

IMPERIAL	AMERICAN
¼ pint cider	⅔ cup cider
4 tablespoons lemon juice	⅓ cup lemon juice
1 teaspoon soft brown sugar	1 teaspoon soft brown sugar
4 tablespoons honey	⅓ cup honey
pinch nutmeg	pinch nutmeg

Mix all the ingredients together. Use to marinate chicken, pork or ham, and use to baste during cooking. Suitable for joints or small cuts.

Spicy mustard marinade

IMPERIAL	AMERICAN
1 tablespoon corn oil	1 tablespoon corn oil
½ pint orange juice	1¼ cups orange juice
2 tablespoons lemon juice	3 tablespoons lemon juice
¼ pint tomato ketchup	⅔ cup tomato catsup
2 tablespoons demerara sugar	3 tablespoons brown sugar
½ teaspoon ground ginger	½ teaspoon ground ginger
pinch cayenne pepper	pinch cayenne pepper
2 teaspoons French mustard	2 teaspoons French mustard
salt to taste	salt to taste

Mix all the ingredients in a saucepan, bring to the boil very slowly, stirring and simmer for 2–3 minutes. Cool before using as a marinade for meat before cooking and to baste with during cooking.

Lamb kebabs*

IMPERIAL	AMERICAN
1 small onion	1 small onion
1 tablespoon wine vinegar	1 tablespoon wine vinegar
1 tablespoon soya sauce	1 tablespoon soy sauce
1 tablespoon corn oil	1 tablespoon corn oil
1 teaspoon salt	1 teaspoon salt
¼ teaspoon pepper	¼ teaspoon pepper
1 teaspoon brown sugar	1 teaspoon brown sugar
½ teaspoon oregano	½ teaspoon oregano
½ teaspoon Tabasco sauce	½ teaspoon Tabasco sauce
1 10-oz. can pineapple cubes	1 10-oz. can pineapple cubes
1 lb. leg of lamb, boned	1 lb. boneless lamb leg
8 oz. button mushrooms, halved	½ lb. button mushrooms, halved

Peel and chop the onion and mix with the next eight ingredients. Drain pineapple and add 2 tablespoons (U.S. 3 tablespoons) syrup to the marinade. Dice the lamb and place in a shallow bowl. Spoon over the marinade, cover and leave to marinate in a cool place for at least 2 hours. Thread the lamb on to skewers, alternating with the halved mushrooms and pieces of pineapple. Place the loaded skewers under a hot grill and cook, turning several times and brushing with the marinade, for 8–10 minutes, or until the lamb is cooked to your taste. Serve on a bed of buttered boiled rice.

* To freeze, pack *uncooked* meat in the marinade, in a plastic container with a seal. Allow a ½-inch headspace for expansion of liquid. To serve allow to defrost, covered in the refrigerator. Cook as for freshly-marinated meat.

Peel and chop the onion and mix with the other ingredients for the marinade. Drain the pineapple and add 2 tablespoons syrup to the marinade.

Dice the lamb and place in a shallow bowl. Spoon over the marinade, cover and leave to marinate in a cool place for at least 2 hours.

Thread the lamb on to skewers, alternating with the halved mushrooms and pineapple cubes. Brush with the marinade and grill.

Stuffings

These can be used in various ways, not only to add flavour to meat but to extend it and make a more economical meal. The type of stuffing is varied according to the meat – a moist stuffing for dry meats such as breast of veal or a dry stuffing for a fat meat such as breast of lamb. The basic ingredient, usually breadcrumbs, is intended to absorb the juices of the meat and to expand during cooking so stuffed joints should never be too tightly tied. The inclusion of an egg produces a firm stuffing which helps to hold the meat together. Where there is no egg or very little liquid in the recipe, stuffings tend to be crumbly and difficult to serve.

Packet stuffings, being made with dried breadcrumbs, require the addition of more liquid and a longer standing period before the stuffing is used, than if you make up your own stuffing with fresh white breadcrumbs. For a more exotic touch, part of the water recommended can be substituted by heated cider, beer or wine. Breadcrumbs may be replaced by cooked potato, rice or dry oatmeal. For white meats with little flavour, sausage meat, which contains some bread, makes an acceptable stuffing; mix with chopped parsley and mixed herbs to flavour.

Recipes for various stuffings are given throughout the book but here is a chart of variations based on packet stuffings:

Basic stuffing	Type of meat	Additions
Sage and onion	Veal, pork	Nutmeg, grated cheese
		Diced apple, prunes
		Chopped ham
Parsley and thyme	Lamb, beef, veal	Chopped bacon, diced onion
		Grated lemon or orange zest
		Diced canned red pimentos
Apple and lemon	Lamb, pork	Chopped mint, chives
		Diced celery
		Diced mushrooms
Onion and mushroom	Beef, lamb	Diced dried apricots
		Chopped walnuts
		Chopped boiled chestnuts

The chopped kidney of the animal can always be included in the stuffing for a joint.

Five ways to use stuffing

1 A joint that has been boned to leave a cavity should be stuffed and loosely tied back into the natural shape; if the meat opens out flat, it should be spread with the stuffing, lightly rolled and tied.
2 Small cuts such as chops and steaks can be slit through the centre, to form pockets, or, beaten out thinly, spread with stuffing and rolled like miniature joints. Pockets should be secured with a wooden cocktail stick during cooking and rolls should be tied with thread which can be easily snipped with scissors and removed.
3 The stuffing mixture can be formed into balls with floured hands and baked on a greased baking sheet, or round the joint in a roasting pan.
4 Packet stuffing mixes can be used to coat meat for frying instead of plain breadcrumbs, or the meat can be brushed with melted fat, grilled on one side, turned and topped with a coating of stuffing sprinkled with grated cheese. Grill until brown.
5 Stuffing mixtures can be added to minced raw meat to make well-flavoured meat loaves or rissoles, or used dry to thicken soups and stews.

Stuffing for pork For a 3 lb. joint, combine 8 oz. pork sausage meat, 1 chopped onion, lightly fried, 2 teaspoons chopped parsley, 8 oz. chopped cooked spinach, 1 egg, salt, pepper and grated nutmeg to taste.

Stuffing for beef For 1½ lb. beef olives, combine 4 oz. (U.S. 2 cups) fresh white breadcrumbs, 2 oz. (U.S. scant ½ cup finely chopped suet) shredded suet, 2 tablespoons (U.S. 3 tablespoons) chopped parsley, 1 tablespoon fresh chopped sweet herbs such as marjoram or thyme, 1 teaspoon grated lemon zest, ¼ teaspoon grated nutmeg, 1 egg, salt and pepper to taste and a little boiling water to mix.

Stuffing for lamb For a 3 lb. joint, combine 4 oz. (U.S. scant 1 cup) cooked long-grain rice, 1 teaspoon curry powder, 1 tablespoon chopped raisins, 1 tablespoon chopped almonds, 1 teaspoon ground coriander, 1 egg, salt and pepper to taste.

Herby liver and mushrooms

IMPERIAL	AMERICAN
2 oz. dripping	¼ cup drippings
1 onion, finely chopped	1 onion, finely chopped
1 lb. pig's liver, cut into strips	1 lb. pork liver, cut into strips
1 teaspoon mixed herbs	1 teaspoon mixed herbs
1 teaspoon chopped parsley	1 teaspoon chopped parsley
2 teaspoons lemon juice	2 teaspoons lemon juice
4 oz. mushrooms, sliced	¼ lb. mushrooms, sliced
¼ pint beef stock	⅔ cup beef stock

Melt the dripping and sauté the onion lightly. Add the liver and seal on all sides. Place half the liver and onions in an ovenproof casserole. Mix together the mixed herbs, parsley and lemon juice and sprinkle over the casserole, then add a layer of mushrooms. Repeat with another layer of liver and onions and end with a layer of mushrooms. Pour in the stock, cover and cook in a moderately hot oven, 375°F, 190°C, Gas Mark 5, for 45 minutes.

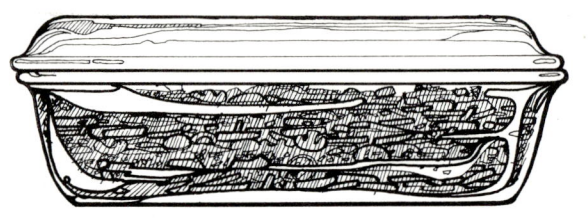

Honey and herb-stuffed veal

IMPERIAL	AMERICAN
Stuffing:	*Stuffing:*
1 4-oz. can red pimentos	1 4-oz. can red pimientos
3 oz. fresh white breadcrumbs	1½ cups fresh soft bread crumbs
grated zest and juice 1 lemon	grated zest and juice 1 lemon
1 teaspoon dried thyme	1 teaspoon dried thyme
1 teaspoon clear honey	1 teaspoon clear honey
salt and pepper to taste	salt and pepper to taste
1 egg, lightly beaten	1 egg, lightly beaten
1 loin of veal, boned	1 boneless veal loin
Sauce:	*Sauce:*
1 tablespoon clear honey	1 tablespoon clear honey
1 oz. butter, melted	2 tablespoons butter, melted
1 teaspoon Worcestershire sauce	1 teaspoon Worcestershire sauce
½ teaspoon dried thyme	½ teaspoon dried thyme
2 teaspoons cornflour	2 teaspoons cornstarch

Drain and chop the pimentos, reserving liquid for sauce. Mix them with the breadcrumbs, zest and juice of lemon, herbs, honey and seasoning. Add sufficient egg to bind and use to stuff the pocket in the veal. Tie neatly and weigh. To make the sauce, mix honey, butter, liquid from pimentos, Worcestershire sauce and herbs and brush over the joint. Place joint in a roasting pan, brush veal with sauce and pour remaining sauce round and roast as per the roasting chart on page 9. Remove joint on to a warm serving dish and keep hot. Moisten cornflour with a little cold water and use to make a thick sauce with the juices in the pan. Serve meat garnished with watercress and surrounded with mounds of cooked rice mixed with cooked peas (made by packing rice mixture into small oiled cups and turning out). Serve the sauce separately.

Make the stuffing and spoon into the pocket in the veal. Tie the joint and weigh it. Make the sauce with the honey, butter, pimento liquid, Worcestershire sauce and herbs.

Place the joint in a roasting pan and brush with the prepared sauce; pour the remaining sauce round the joint and roast according to the chart.

Thicken juices in the pan with blended cornflour. Serve the veal garnished with watercress and rice moulds made by packing cooked peas and rice in oiled cups and turning out.

Sauces and soups

Barbecue sauce Fry 1 large chopped onion in $\frac{1}{2}$ oz. (U.S. 1 tablespoon) dripping for 4 minutes. Add 4 tablespoons (U.S. $\frac{1}{3}$ cup) water, 2 tablespoons (U.S. 3 tablespoons) soft brown sugar, 3 tablespoons (U.S. scant $\frac{1}{4}$ cup) vinegar, 1 teaspoon Worcestershire sauce, $\frac{1}{2}$ teaspoon salt, pinch cayenne pepper, 2 teaspoons dry mustard, pinch dried mixed herbs, 2$\frac{1}{4}$-oz. can (U.S. $\frac{1}{4}$ cup) tomato purée and a pinch of powdered garlic. Bring to the boil, stirring constantly, and simmer gently for 10 minutes.

Béchamel sauce To 1 pint (U.S. 2$\frac{1}{2}$ cups) milk in a saucepan, add $\frac{1}{2}$ carrot and $\frac{1}{2}$ onion, roughly chopped, together with 2 peppercorns, 1 bay leaf and a pinch of mace. Bring slowly to the boil, remove from heat and allow to stand for 10 minutes, then strain. Melt 2 oz. (U.S. $\frac{1}{4}$ cup) butter in a saucepan, stir in 2 oz. (U.S. $\frac{1}{2}$ cup) flour and cook without browning for 3 minutes. Gradually add the flavoured milk and bring to the boil, stirring constantly, until thickened and then season to taste with salt and pepper.

Variations: *Cream sauce* To the basic sauce add $\frac{1}{4}$ pint (U.S. $\frac{2}{3}$ cup) cream. *Sauce mornay* To the basic sauce add 2 egg yolks and 2 oz. (U.S. $\frac{1}{2}$ cup) grated cheese. *Onion sauce* To the basic sauce add 1 large onion, chopped and boiled for 5 minutes in a little water then drained and sautéed lightly in 1 oz. (U.S. 2 tablespoons) butter. Simmer sauce for 15 minutes. If you prefer a smooth texture, purée before serving, with lamb or veal. *Caper sauce* Stir 2 tablespoons (U.S. 3 tablespoons) drained capers into 1 pint (U.S. 2$\frac{1}{2}$ cups) basic sauce.

Brown sauce Melt 2 tablespoons (U.S. 3 tablespoons) dripping in a saucepan and add 2 chopped carrots, 1 sliced onion, 2 chopped sticks of celery and sauté until the vegetables are beginning to brown. Sprinkle in 2 tablespoons (U.S. 3 tablespoons) flour and cook gently until well browned. Add 1 pint (U.S. 2$\frac{1}{2}$ cups) beef stock, a bouquet garni and 2 tablespoons (U.S. 3 tablespoons) tomato purée. Cook, stirring frequently, until thickened. Simmer over low heat for at least 1 hour, strain and correct seasoning. If necessary, reduce slightly to thicken.

Variations: *Sauce bordelaise* Finely chop 2 shallots and cook in $\frac{1}{4}$ pint (U.S. $\frac{2}{3}$ cup) red wine until soft and the wine is reduced by a third then add to the basic sauce and heat through before serving. *Espagnole sauce* Sauté 2 oz. (U.S. $\frac{1}{4}$ cup) chopped ham, 2 oz. (U.S. $\frac{1}{4}$ cup) chopped mushrooms in a little butter and add to the sauce with 4 tablespoons (U.S. $\frac{1}{3}$ cup) dry sherry. Espagnole sauce is a perfect partner to chops, steaks, sweetbreads and kidneys.

Cumberland sauce Blanch the rind of ½ a lemon and ½ an orange and cut into strips. Add 3 tablespoons (U.S. scant ¼ cup) redcurrant jelly, ½ teaspoon dry mustard, lemon juice to taste, ¼ pint (U.S. ⅔ cup) red wine or port and stir over low heat until well blended.

Horseradish sauce (hot) Melt 1½ oz. (U.S. 3 tablespoons) butter in a small saucepan and add 2 teaspoons dry mustard and 1½ oz. (U.S. 6 tablespoons) flour. Stir well then add 1 pint (U.S. 2½ cups) milk or stock and bring to the boil, stirring. Cook for 5 minutes and then add 1 teaspoon sugar, 1 teaspoon salt, 6 tablespoons (U.S. ½ cup) vinegar and about 4½ oz. (U.S. ¾ cup) grated horseradish. The quantity of horseradish can be varied according to taste.

Horseradish sauce (cold) Mix together 1½ oz. (U.S. ¼ cup) finely grated horseradish, 4 tablespoons (U.S. ⅓ cup) single cream, 1 tablespoon vinegar, 2 teaspoons castor sugar and a pinch of salt. Colour slightly with a little mustard.

Variation: For a slightly different flavour, try using ¼ pint (U.S. ⅔ cup) soured cream instead of cream; into this stir 1 tablespoon grated horseradish, ½ teaspoon made mustard and seasoning. Allow to stand at least 1 hour before serving with hot or cold roast beef.

Mint sauce Combine 4 tablespoons (U.S. ⅓ cup) wine or malt vinegar with 4 tablespoons (U.S. ⅓ cup) chopped fresh mint and 1 tablespoon of sugar. Stir until the sugar has dissolved and leave for 2 hours.

Variation: Cider instead of vinegar mixed with the chopped mint and sugar makes a complementary blend of flavours to serve with lamb.

Mustard sauce In a small basin mix together 1 tablespoon made mustard, 1 tablespoon sugar and 2 tablespoons (U.S. 3 tablespoons) vinegar. Gradually add ¼ pint (U.S. ⅔ cup) oil, stirring continually. Add a little chopped parsley before serving with cold roast beef and salad.

Tomato sauce Melt 1½ oz. (U.S. 3 tablespoons) butter in a large pan and fry 1 large finely chopped onion and 1 crushed clove of garlic in this until lightly browned. Stir in 1½ oz. (U.S. 6 tablespoons) flour and cook, stirring constantly, until golden. Add a 5-oz. can (U.S. ½ cup) tomato purée, 1 pint (U.S. 2½ cups) beef stock, 1 teaspoon dried mixed herbs, 1 teaspoon sugar, seasoning and a bay leaf. Bring to the boil, stirring constantly until thickened. Cover and simmer gently for 25 minutes.

Gravy Pour off the fat leaving a little in the roasting pan. Remove from the heat and stir in 2 tablespoons (U.S. 3 tablespoons) flour or 1 tablespoon cornflour. Mix well, place over heat and cook, stirring until the mixture begins to bubble. Add ½ pint (U.S. 1¼ cups) stock, stir until boiling and cook for a few minutes.

Or, use gravy powder as the thickening agent, in which case stir 1 tablespoon powder into sufficient cold water to moisten, add ½ pint (U.S. 1¼ cups) stock or water and stir into the pan juices. Bring to the boil, stirring, and cook for a few minutes. All gravies look better if poured into the serving boat through a strainer but this is not essential.

Note: Where stock cubes made up with water are substituted for bone stock, it is advisable to use beef stock cubes for dark meats and sauces, and chicken stock cubes for white meats and light-coloured sauces. (Remember stock cubes are well seasoned.)

Consommé

IMPERIAL	AMERICAN
4 pints beef stock	10 cups beef stock
1 onion, chopped	1 onion, chopped
1 carrot, chopped	1 carrot, chopped
1 bay leaf	1 bay leaf
salt and pepper to taste	salt and pepper to taste
1 egg white, stiffly beaten	1 egg white, stiffly beaten
1 egg shell	1 egg shell
¼ pint sherry	⅔ cup sherry

Put stock into a saucepan with the onion, carrot and bay leaf. Bring to the boil, taste and adjust seasoning. Simmer gently for 1 hour then strain carefully through several thicknesses of muslin. To clear the consommé, return to the pan and add the egg white and egg shell. Bring to the boil and simmer for a further 20 minutes then re-strain and add the sherry. (*Serves 8.*)

Variation: To make *consommé Célestine* add 2 large thin pancakes cut into fine strips as a garnish. Reheat gently in the consommé before serving.

Scotch broth

IMPERIAL	AMERICAN
1 lb. scrag end of neck of lamb	1 lb. lamb neck slices
2 oz. pearl barley	about ¼ cup pearl barley
3 pints water	7½ cups water
salt and pepper to taste	salt and pepper to taste
2 onions, chopped	2 onions, chopped
2 carrots, chopped	2 carrots, chopped
2 sticks celery, chopped	2 stalks celery, chopped
2 tablespoons chopped parsley	3 tablespoons chopped parsley

Trim the meat removing as much fat as possible and place in a large saucepan together with the barley, water and seasoning. Bring to the boil, cover and simmer for 2 hours, over very low heat, removing any grey scum that forms. Strain and carefully remove all bones. Place meat, vegetables and stock in pan, bring to the boil and simmer for a further 1½ hours. Serve sprinkled with chopped parsley.

Kidney soup

IMPERIAL	AMERICAN
1 oz. dripping	2 tablespoons drippings
8 oz. ox kidney, in small pieces	½ lb. beef kidney, in small pieces
1 onion, sliced	1 onion, sliced
1 oz. flour	¼ cup all-purpose flour
2 pints beef stock	5 cups beef stock
2 carrots, diced	2 carrots, diced
2 sticks celery, chopped	2 stalks celery, chopped
1 sprig parsley	1 sprig parsley
1 bay leaf	1 bay leaf
pinch ground mace	pinch ground mace
salt and pepper to taste	salt and pepper to taste

Melt the dripping and sauté the kidney lightly. Remove from pan. Fry onion and flour gently until well browned then stir in the stock. Bring to the boil, stirring constantly, until thickened. Replace the kidneys, vegetables, parsley and seasonings and simmer gently for about 2 hours. Strain soup, add a little finely chopped kidney and adjust seasoning.

Mulligatawny soup

IMPERIAL	AMERICAN
2 oz. dripping	¼ cup drippings
2 onions, chopped	2 onions, chopped
1 large carrot, chopped	1 large carrot, chopped
1 apple, chopped	1 apple, chopped
1 oz. flour	¼ cup all-purpose flour
1 tablespoon curry powder	1 tablespoon curry powder
2 pints lamb or mutton stock	5 cups lamb or mutton stock
1 tablespoon chutney	1 tablespoon chutney
pinch sugar	pinch sugar
1 oz. sultanas	3 tablespoons seedless white raisins
salt and pepper to taste	salt and pepper to taste

Melt the dripping in a saucepan and sauté the vegetables until softened. Stir in the flour and curry powder and cook over gentle heat for a few minutes. Gradually add the stock, bring to the boil, stirring constantly until thickened. Add the chutney, sugar, sultanas and seasoning. Return to the boil and simmer for about 1 hour. Either liquidise the soup or rub through a sieve; reheat and adjust seasoning. A little extra sugar, vinegar or lemon juice may be added at this stage, to enhance the flavour. For a mild flavour, reduce curry powder by half.

Garnishes

The most important purpose of a garnish is to enhance the dish by giving a colour contrast and the flavour should also be in keeping with the dish itself.

Parsley This can be used in two ways, either in the form of sprigs or finely chopped for sprinkling. There are two varieties of parsley, one of which has tight frilly leaves. The looser leafed variety is only suitable for chopping.

Herbs Other sweet herbs, particularly chervil and chives look and taste effective when chopped and sprinkled over rich meat dishes.

Lemon This is used in many ways, the most usual being lemon quarters or wedges obtained by cutting the fruit into eight. Lemon waterlilies are made by making diagonal cuts through to the centre all round the middle of the lemon in a zig-zag pattern, then pulling the two halves apart. An alternative is to cut off the top third of the lemon, remove a small slice from the base so it will stand firmly, and begin peeling round the cut edge until the strip of peel can be tied in a single knot. Thin slices, overlapping, are also used, and a lemon fan is made by cutting through a slice just to the centre, then giving a twist. A lemon butterfly is made by cutting a slice completely in half, then cutting through each half to the centre point, spreading it out to form a butterfly shape still joined at the centre. A sprinkling of coarsely grated lemon zest is also sometimes used. A lemon basket is made by cutting two parallel lines over the top and through to the centre, then slicing out round the middle, up to the two cuts, entirely removing two wedges from the lemon. The flesh under the handle is also removed with a sharp pointed knife and the basket either left empty or filled with a bunch of parsley.

Orange All the garnishes listed for lemons can be made with oranges instead. To garnish duck, orange slices sometimes have the peel removed and the juicy edge of the orange coated in chopped parsley.

Eggs Wedges and slices of hard-boiled egg add a good touch of colour. Sometimes the yolk is scooped out and the dish is garnished with alternate piles of the chopped white and sieved yolk. Or the yolk can be mixed with spices such as curry powder, savoury sauces and herbs and piled or piped back inside the empty cases. A slice of egg can be topped with a curled anchovy, a few capers or a small spoonful of caviar.

Carrots Cooked carrots, cut across in thin slices look most effective if the slices are stamped out with a miniature cocktail cutter with a fancy edge.

Olives Stuffed olives, sliced across, give a colourful finish to veal dishes. Black olives should be stoned, the empty halves pressed down flat, skin side uppermost and cut into diamonds.

Tomatoes A simple garnish can be made with overlapping tomato slices. Tomato waterlilies are made in the same way as lemon waterlilies. Tomato cups are hollowed out and the centres filled with a mixed vegetable salad to garnish cold dishes or a rice or spinach stuffing for hot dishes. Sometimes the top which has been sliced off is neatly trimmed and replaced at an angle. Tomato toadstools are good with an assortment of cold meats. Slice the bottom of a hard-boiled egg so that it will stand upright. Cut a tomato in half, scoop out most of the pulp and place tomato case skin-side uppermost on top of the egg. Garnish with piped dots of mayonnaise.

Gherkins A gherkin fan is made by cutting through in parallel slices from the tip almost to the base. Fan out the slices evenly. Fairly large gherkins can be sliced and stamped out in the same way as carrot slices.

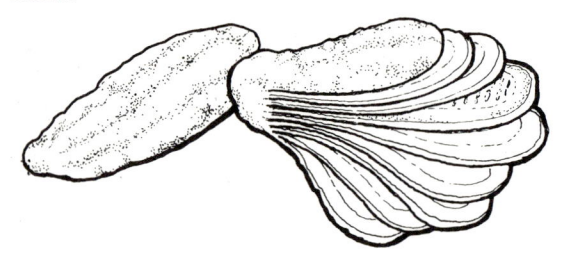

Paprika pepper A sprinkling of paprika pepper falls more evenly if it comes from a shaker or is sieved over the food, and gives a splendid touch of colour to rice, soured cream or mayonnaise.

Radishes These can be cut to make roses by slicing through the centre almost to the base four or more times according to the size of the radish. Put into iced water for an hour to open out. A differently shaped rose is made by cutting two parallel slits and then another two at right-angles, leaving the square centre of the radish uncut.

Red and green peppers Thin strips or circles of fresh pepper can be used to enclose bundles of asparagus tips. Canned red pepper, well drained, can be cut into fancy shapes as black olives.

Watercress Sprigs, varying in size, are used for almost any meat dish and large sprigs are particularly useful to circle the base of a joint on the serving dish.

Croûtons Thin slices of stale white bread, with the crusts removed, can be cut in large triangles to place round the outside of a casserole dish or small triangles or cubes sprinkled over a cooked meat dish or soup. Fry in bacon fat, good meat dripping, or a mixture of butter and oil until just golden brown.

Fleurons Odd pieces of pastry, preferably puff pastry, can be cut out with a small circular cutter into crescent shapes by moving the cutter along a fraction of an inch. When baked they provide crescent, moon and leaf shapes for garnishing.

Cucumber This makes the classic garnish for all cold meats. Thin slices from a peeled or unpeeled cucumber are arranged overlapping in circles or as a border. The dark green skin can be scored with a fork or channelled with a *cannel* knife so that when the cucumber is sliced it has a fancy edge. Slices of cucumber can be slit through to the centre and used to make twists or cones. Cucumber cups, made by cutting 1-inch chunks and hollowing them out, look effective filled with cooked peas; or cucumber boats – 2-inch lengths, hollowed out along the length are usually filled with mixed vegetable salad or cottage or cream cheese – either plain or flavoured.

Wines for the table and meat cookery

Wine is the perfect partner to food. The pleasure of drinking wine with a meal is one which people are enjoying far more frequently at home. Holidays abroad perhaps are responsible. One soon learns to appreciate the immense difference a glass of wine makes to even a modest meal. And when there is a little left in the bottle this is an encouragement to begin learning how to cook with wine. A surprisingly small amount can transform a meat dish. It imparts a richer flavour to delicate dishes and a mellow roundness to the more robust meats. If you hesitate actually to buy wine for cooking, make your first experiment with those dishes which call for cider or beer.

What to serve There is no mystique about matching the wine to the food. Generally speaking one serves a red wine with red meats, such as beef and lamb, and a white wine with light meats such as veal and pork. A happy compromise which suits most tastes is a rosé. However, people are less affected nowadays by the sort of snobbery which made these hard and fast rules difficult to flout, and drink the wines they prefer. Of course a dish cooked with wine will be perfectly complemented by wine to drink of the same colour, and from the same district. Wines for the table need not be expensive. Choose a full-bodied dry red wine, for example, a young, strong Beaujolais, Mâcon among the Burgundies, or a claret such as St. Emilion. An Italian Chianti or Hungarian Bull's Blood would be interesting alternatives. French Tavel or Rosé d'Anjou have a strong competitor in the Portuguese sparkling Mateus Rosé. A sparkling white wine such as Veuve du Vernay adds elegance to any occasion and need not break the bank. The white Burgundies with their cool dry crispness are also popular. Pouilly, Pouilly Fuissé and if you can afford it Chablis are sure to please. Muscadet or Vouvray deserve more recognition. From Italy try Orvieto Secco, or Abboccato if you like a sweeter wine. Other popular white wines are the fresh tasting Vinho Verdes from Portugal, German Liebfraumilch and Yugoslavian Riesling. If you can, drink Château or Domaine bottled wines.

How to serve Keep the bottles in a rack, or at least horizontal so that the corks do not dry out. The temperature of the wine is more important than the shape of the glass. However, the traditional shapes have evolved to suit the wines one serves in them. White wines should be served chilled, and this can be achieved by placing the bottle in the door of the refrigerator an hour before serving, or wrapping a napkin wrung out in cold water round the bottle. Open only a few minutes before serving and never add ice to wine in the glass. Rosé wines should be served slightly chilled. Serve red wines *chambré* or at room temperature. They should also be opened for at least an hour before being drunk. But do not put the bottle near a fire or in hot water. Just remove the cork and place the bottle in a warm room until warm to the touch. Fine red wines should be poured steadily, and not right down to the lees, as there may be sediment at the bottom, especially if the bottle has not been stood upright for a period of about 48 hours. For this reason, fine wine is often decanted, to make pouring out at the table easier. To do this, pour the wine steadily into a warm, dry carafe with a light behind the bottle (*à la bougie*, or against candle-light is the French way of describing this rather charming ceremony), stopping as soon as the remaining wine looks cloudy. Put the lighted candle in a fairly tall candlestick, or a small table light with the shade removed, about four inches to the right of the carafe and hold the bottle as you pour so that the light comes just behind the base of the neck. It is often necessary to wipe the neck of the bottle before you begin. Decant a young red Bordeaux wine as early as possible before the meal but a really mature wine only shortly beforehand. Young red Burgundies need only be decanted, or the cork removed, one hour before the meal.

When pouring out wine, leave at least an inch space below the rim of the glass to allow the wine to 'breathe'. Never fill to brimming point. Chilled wine should be served in a long stemmed glass so that the hand does not touch the bowl, and warm the wine. Red wine is served in a goblet shaped glass with a short stem, so that the hand clasps the bowl and warms it. For sparkling wines, the wide, coupe-shaped glass is less used today than a tulip-shaped glass, which retains the sparkle longer.

How to use in cooking Most housewives use leftovers, or part of a bottle of red opened in advance of the meal for the table. A cheap cooking wine which is thin, too dry or lacking body and flavour is just as disappointing in the finished dish as in the glass.

Do not leave small quantities in the bottom of a large bottle. Transfer to a small bottle, which you keep for the purpose, with a clean cork or plastic bottle cap and use up within a fortnight. Red wine may have a spoonful of brandy or any fortified wine added to extend its life. White wine (which can be stored in the refrigerator) keeps a little longer, especially if you add a spoonful of white vermouth or dry sherry. Do not mix red and white. As a general rule medium dry wines which are good for drinking with meat dishes are good for meat cookery. Fortified wines have a higher percentage of proof spirit and more concentrated flavour. They have had brandy added and keep indefinitely if tightly corked, so you can always have them to hand when cooking. A dry sherry or Madeira is the most complementary to the flavour of meat. Still dry cider goes well with beef, a medium sweet cider is more acceptable with pork, lamb and veal. Beer, from pale ale to dark brown, goes particularly well with beef.

How to flamber Flaming meat with spirit consumes both the alcohol and excess fat in the meat, emphasising the basic flavour of the spirit used. Brandy, being based on the grape, is the best choice if wine is then added, although whisky is also occasionally used for meat dishes. Fortified wines will also flame, but the flavour which remains behind is much milder, and liqueurs are on the whole too sweet for meat cookery. To ensure that the spirit will flame, warm it carefully in a small saucepan, ignite it at arm's length and pour at once over the meat. The flames will leap to a dramatic height only if there is a lot of surplus fat in the dish which ignites. A tiny sprinkling of sugar over the food ensures a bright flame, but a taste of caramel may result, which is only pleasant in dishes where a pinch of sugar might be added to bring out the flavour of the sauce, as it might be if tomato is used. Keep shaking the pan gently and spooning the liquid over the food as long as the flames last. Although this may be carried out just before the dish is served, many classic recipes require it to be done at the beginning of the cooking period and wine also to be added to the sauce. Long cooking after flaming mellows and refines the taste.

Fast cooking dishes It is essential that wine added to a dish should be cooked sufficiently to drive off the alcohol content. For quickly cooked dishes such as grilled or fried steaks, the meat is best cooked until just done, then removed and the wine added to the juices in the pan and cooked at a rapid boil until reduced to a small quantity. Extra butter, or beurre manié may be added to thicken the sauce. For a very rich flavour, thicken by stirring in a few spoonfuls of double cream. Reduction is quicker if the pan has a wide surface – a shallow frying pan is ideal. Kebabs can be placed in a wine marinade before grilling.

Slow cooking dishes Less tender cuts to be stewed, cooked en casserole or braised, are tenderised and permeated with a much richer flavour, if wine is added to the stock. All the alcohol will vanish during the long slow cooking, and only the essential flavour of the wine remains. Roasting joints should be basted with wine during cooking, and the juices surrounding the meat will provide an interesting sauce.

Index

Apple:
  Liver and apple hot-pot 47
  Roast pork with carnival apples 62
  Stuffed baked apples 45
Apricot:
  Stuffed lamb shoulder with apricot cups 54
  Worcester fruited pork 52
Automatic oven menus 45

Bacon:
  Braised liver and bacon 48, 69
Barbecue sauce 73
Barbecued lamb 35
Béchamel sauce 73
Beef:
  Buying for the freezer 15
  Carving beef 24
  Carving cooked beef joints (U.S. edition) 24
  Carving steaks (U.S. edition) 24
  Cuts of beef 22–3
  Defrosting beef 16
  How to choose beef 21
  Offal from beef 21
  Preparing steaks 24
  Roasting chart 9
  Roasting chart for frozen beef 10
  Variety meats (U.S. edition) 21
Beef recipes
  Beef chain with an economy cut 36
  Beef and chestnut ragoût 37
  Beef chop suey 50
  Beef Marguerite 36
  Beef olives in mushroom sauce 66
  Beef sauerbraten 39
  Beef in spiced cider 38
  Beef-stuffed peppers 67
  Beef tea 69
  Bobotee 67
  Boeuf carbonnade 52
  Boeuf en croûte 57
  Boiled beef and carrots 38
  Chilli con carne 38
  Cold spiced beef 53
  Cornish pasties 68
  Curried mince with watercress salad 53
  Daube marseillaise 53
  Devonshire meat loaf 35
  Duchess mince 36
  Family beefburgers 37
  Fondue bourguignonne 56
  Ilchester beef cobbler 41
  Meatballs in mustard sauce 40
  Mince and mushroom crumble 36
  Pot-roast of brisket 38
  Potted beef 65
  Potted hough 34
  Raw beef sandwiches 69
  Rich beef stew with mustard croûtons 58
  Rinderrouladen 56
  Steak, kidney and mushroom pie 54
  Steak and kidney pudding 34
  Stuffing for beef 72
  Wineseller's beefsteak 66
Blender pâtés 65
Bobotee 67
Boeuf carbonnade 52
Boeuf en croûte 57
Boiled beef and carrots 38
Boiling meat 8
Brains:
  Brains in black butter 62
  Calves brains 17
  Lamb's brains 25
Braised liver and bacon 48, 69
Braising meat 8
Brown sauce 73
Bulk buying for the freezer 15–16

Calf's foot broth 69
Caper sauce 73
Carrots as garnish 76
Casseroles and stews:
  To casserole meat 9
  Basic lamb stew 41
  Boeuf carbonnade 52
  Country pork casserole 46
  Daube marseillaise 53
  Greek lamb stew 42
  Irish stew 42
  Lamb with haricot beans 42
  Lamb printanière 41
  Lemon lamb casserole 45
  Liver and apple hot-pot 47
  Navarin of lamb 44
  Piquant pork stew with parsley and lemon dumplings 46
  Rich beef stew with mustard croûtons 58
  Spring veal casserole 33
  Stewed oxtail 40
  Veal and marrow casserole 33
Celery, braised 45
Cheek 21
Cheesy-stuffed tomatoes 66
Chilli con carne 38
Cider marinade 70
Consommé 74
Cornish pasties 68

Country pork casserole 46
Courgettes, steak-stuffed 67
Cream sauce 73
Creamed sweetbreads with mushrooms 62
Croûtons 58, 76
Crown roast of lamb 64
Cucumber as garnish 76
Cumberland kidneys 68
Cumberland sauce 74
Curried dishes:
  Curried mince with watercress salad 53
  Korma kebabs 58
  Madras curry 42
  Cutlets à la milanaise 60

Daube marseillaise 53
Defrosting, tips for 16
Devonshire meat loaf 35
Duchess mince 36
Dumplings:
  Parsley and lemon dumplings 46

Eggs as garnish 76
Escalopes de veau meunière 50
Espagnole sauce 73

Faggots 48
Family beefburgers 37
Feet 17
Flamber, how to 78
Fleurons 76
Fondue bourguignonne 56
Freezer, bulk buying for the 15–16
Freezer, wrapping for the 16
Fricassée of lamb 54
Frying meat 9

Garnishes 75–6
Gherkins as garnish 76
Gravy 74
Greek lamb stew 42
Grilled sausages and pineapple 66
Grilling meat 9
Guernsey creamed tripe 48

Ham:
  To score ham (U.S. edition) 32
  Pork and ham risotto 43
Head:
  Calf's head 17
  Pig's head 29
  Sheep's head 25
Heart:
  Calf's heart 17
  Lamb's heart 25
  Ox heart 21
  Stuffed ox heart 48
Heel 21
Herbs 11–12
Herby liver and mushrooms 72
Holiday barbecued lamb 35
Honey and herb-stuffed veal 72

Horseradish sauce, hot or cold 74
Ilchester beef cobbler 41
Invalid dishes 69
Irish stew 42
Kebabs:
  Korma kebabs 58
  Lamb kebabs 70
  Pork and pear kebabs 58
Kidney:
  Calves kidneys 17
  Cumberland kidneys 68
  Kidney soup 75
  Lamb's kidneys 25
  Ox kidney 21
  Pig's kidneys 29
  Rognons sautés au vin rouge 62
  Steak, kidney and mushroom pie 54
  Steak and kidney pudding 34
Lamb:
  Bulk buying for the freezer 15
  Carving cooked joints of lamb (U.S. edition) 28
  Carving lamb 28
  Cuts of lamb 26–7
  Defrosting lamb 16
  How to choose lamb 25
  Offal from lamb 25
  Roasting chart 9
  Roasting chart for frozen lamb 10
  Variety meats (U.S. edition) 25
  Various uses for cuts of lamb (U.S. edition) 25–6
  Various uses for cuts of lamb 26
Lamb recipes
  Basic lamb stew 41
  Breast of lamb with thyme stuffing 44
  Crown roast of lamb 64
  Crunchy lamb rissoles 43
  Cutlets à la milanaise 60
  Fricassée of lamb 54
  Greek lamb stew 42
  Holiday barbecued lamb 35
  Irish stew 42
  Korma kebabs 58
  Lamb chain with economy cuts 41
  Lamb with haricot beans 42
  Lamb kebabs 70
  Lamb pilau 67
  Lamb printanière 41
  Lemon lamb casserole 45
  Madras curry 42
  Moussaka 42
  Navarin of lamb 44
  New Zealand guard of honour 64
  Roast lamb with rosemary and garlic 45

79

Stuffed lamb shoulder with apricot cups 54
Stuffing for lamb 72
Lemon garnishes 75
Lemon and honey sauce 45
Lemon lamb casserole 45
Liver:
  Beef liver (U.S. edition) 21
  Braised liver and bacon 48, 69
  Calf's liver 17
  Faggots 48
  Herby liver and mushrooms 72
  Lamb's liver 25
  Liver and apple hot-pot 47
  Ox liver 22
  Pig's liver 29
  Sheep's liver 25
  Yeoman's pâté 65

Madeira sauce 58
Madras curry 42
Marinades 70
Meat and potato soufflé 69
Meatballs in mustard sauce 40
Mince, basic 36
Mince and mushroom crumble 36
Mint sauce 74
Moussaka 42
Mulligatawny soup 75
Mushroom:
  Beef olives in mushroom sauce 66
  Creamed sweetbreads with mushrooms 62
  Mince and mushroom crumble 36
  Steak, kidney and mushroom pie 54
Mustard croûtons 58
Mustard sauce 74

Navarin of lamb 44
New Zealand guard of honour 64

Olives as garnish 76
Onion sauce 73
Orange as garnish 76
Orange honey glaze 50
Oxtail 22
Oxtail, stewed 40

Pans and casseroles 13–14
Paprika pepper as garnish 76
Parsley as garnish 75
Parsley and lemon dumplings 46
Pâtés in the blender 65
Peppers, beef-stuffed 67
Peppers as garnish 76
Pies:
  Steak, kidney and mushroom pie 54
  Veal and corn pie 33
Pocket-stuffed pork chops 60

Pork:
  Buying for the freezer 15
  Carving cooked joints of pork 32
  Cooking methods for cooked joints of pork (U.S. edition) 30
  Cuts of pork 30–31
  Defrosting pork 16
  How to choose pork 29
  Offal from pork 29
  Roasting chart 9
  Roasting chart for frozen pork 10
  Scoring skin for crackling 32
  To pickle 30
  Variety meats (U.S. edition) 29
  Various uses for cuts of pork 29
  Pork recipes
  Country pork casserole 46
  Faggots 48
  Piquant pork stew with parsley and lemon dumplings 46
  Pocket-stuffed pork chops 60
  Pork chops with orange honey glaze 50
  Pork and ham risotto 43
  Pork and leek pudding 35
  Pork loaf 35
  Pork and pear kebabs 58
  Roast belly pork in lemon and honey sauce 45
  Roast pork with carnival apples 62
  Saucy spare ribs 46
  Stuffing for pork 72
  Sweet and sour pork 46
  Tasty pork mince 66
  Worcester fruited pork 52
Potato:
  Baked potatoes with soured cream and chive dressing 45
  Meat and potato soufflé 69
  Roast potatoes 45
Pot-roast of brisket 38
Pot-roasting meat 8
Potted beef 65
Potted hough 34
Pressed ox tongue 61
Pudding:
  Pork and leek pudding 35
  Steak and kidney pudding 34

Radishes as garnish 76
Raw beef sandwiches 69
Rice Josephine 45
Rinderrouladen 56
Risotto of pork and ham 43
Rissoles 43
Roasting:
  Quick roasting 8
  New methods of roasting 39
  Roasting chart 9

Roasting chart for meat from the frozen state 10
Slow roasting 8
Rognons sautés au vin rouge 62
Roulades de veau 49

Sauces:
  Barbecue sauce 73
  Béchamel sauce 73
  Brown sauce 73
  Caper sauce 73
  Cream sauce 73
  Cumberland sauce 74
  Espagnole sauce 73
  Gravy 74
  Horseradish sauce, hot or cold 74
  Lemon and honey sauce 45
  Madeira sauce 58
  Mint sauce 74
  Mustard sauce 74
  Onion sauce 73
  Sauce bordelaise 73
  Sauce mornay 73
  Tomato sauce 74
Saucy spare ribs 46
Sausage:
  Grilled sausages and pineapple 66
  Scotch broth 74
Soufflé:
  Meat and potato soufflé 69
Soup:
  Beef tea 69
  Calf's foot broth 69
  Consommé 74
  Consommé Célestine 74
  Kidney soup 75
  Mulligatawny soup 75
  Scotch broth 74
Spiced beef, cold 53
Spices 12
Spicy mustard marinade 70
Spring veal casserole 33
Steak, kidney and mushroom pie 54
Steak and kidney pudding 34
Steak-stuffed courgettes 67
Stewing meat 9
Stews *see* Casseroles and stews
Storing raw or cooked meat 9
Stuffed baked apples 45
Stuffed lamb shoulder with apricot cups 54
Stuffed loin of veal with pineapple 61
Stuffed ox heart 48
Stuffings:
  Five ways to use stuffing 72
  Stuffing for beef 72
  Stuffing for lamb 72
  Stuffing for pork 72
  Thyme stuffing 44
  Variations on packet stuffings 71
Sweet Malayan veal 49
Sweet and sour pork 46

Sweetbreads:
  Calves sweetbreads 17
  Creamed sweetbreads with mushrooms 62
  Lamb's sweetbreads 25
  Ox sweetbreads 22

Thyme stuffing 44
Tomatoes as garnish 76
  Tomato sauce 74
Tongue:
  Calf's tongue 17
  Lamb's tongue 25
  Ox tongue 22
  Ox tongue with Madeira sauce 58
  Pressed ox tongue 61
  Sheep's tongue 25
Tripe 22:
  Guernsey creamed tripe 48
Trotters 29

Utensils 13

Veal:
  Bulk buying for the freezer 15
  Carving cooked veal joints (U.S. edition) 20
  Carving cuts of veal 20
  Cuts of veal 18–19
  Defrosting veal 16
  How to choose veal 17
  Offal 17
  Preparing stuffed veal cuts 20
  Roasting chart 9
  Roasting chart for frozen veal 10
  Variety meats (U.S. edition) 17
  Various uses for cuts of veal 17–18
  Veal recipes
  Escalopes de veau meunière 50
  Honey and herb-stuffed veal 72
  Potted hough 34
  Roulades de veau 49
  Spring veal casserole 33
  Stuffed loin of veal with pineapple 61
  Sweet Malayan veal 49
  Veal Cordon Bleu 20
  Veal and corn pie 33
  Veal flamenco 50
  Veal and marrow casserole 33

Watercress as garnish 76
Watercress salad 53
Wines, what to serve and how 77
Wines, to use in cooking 77–8
Wineseller's beefsteak 66
Worcester fruited pork 52

Yeoman's pâté 65
Yorkshire pudding 10